Walking Away from Hate

Praise for *Walking Away from Hate*

"Bold, courageous, and brutally honest. Should be required reading in all high schools. The unbearable near-tragedies of this girl's journey and her mother's terror hounded me long after the last page was turned."

DONNA MORRISSEY,
Award-winning author of *The Fortunate Brother* and *Sylvanus Now*

"I've known Lauren—and her story—for some time now, but reading *Walking Away from Hate* sheds new light on her journey. In the conversations between Lauren and her mom Jeanette, we learn valuable lessons about the white supremacist movement, and even more important lessons about the power of love and forgiveness. About the movement, we learn how it is badly riddled with hypocrisy, disloyalty, disrespect and misogyny. About love, we learn that when we offer unconditional love, we have the power to save those around us. Their shared story gives hope that there is a path for others who want to walk away from hate."

DR. BARBARA PERRY,
Director, Centre on Hate, Bias and Extremism, Ontario Tech University

"While the juxtaposition of two worlds is a central theme of this mother/daughter story, equally powerful are the insights into how white extremist thinking is fostered in the young. *Walking Away from Hate* serves as a contrast between ideals of justice, truth and social issues, and ideally will be used for classroom study and parent/child discussions of ideology gone awry and its powerful lure and message for those who grow into adulthood angry about society's failures and parental teachings."

MIDWEST BOOK REVIEW

"Jeanette and Lauren portray the difficult and painful experiences when a child becomes involved in extremism—and how to overcome this. *Walking Away from Hate* is a unique account from a mother and a daughter's parallel experience of radicalization. For professionals, family members and individuals who are leaving their involvement in extremism and hate, this is a highly recommended read."

ROBERT ÖRELL, International expert on the disengagement and reintegration of violent extremists, and former leader of Exit Sweden and Exit USA

Walking Away from Hate

Our Journey through Extremism

by
Jeanette and Lauren Manning

TIDEWATER
PRESS

Published by Tidewater Press
New Westminster, BC, Canada

tidewaterpress.ca
978-1-990160-00-4 (print)
978-1-990160-01-1 (ebook)

LIBRARY AND ARCHIVES CANADA CATALOGUING IN PUBLICATION
Title: Walking away from hate : our journey through extremism / by Jeanette and Lauren Manning.
Names: Manning, Jeanette, author. | Manning, Lauren (Construction worker), author.
Identifiers: Canadiana (print) 20210156759 | Canadiana (ebook) 20210157127 | ISBN 9781990160004 (softcover) | ISBN 9781990160011 (HTML)
Subjects: LCSH: Manning, Lauren (Construction worker) | LCSH: Manning, Jeanette. | LCSH: Right-wing extremists—Canada—Biography. | LCSH: Skinheads—Canada—Biography. | LCSH: White supremacy movements—Canada. | LCSH: Hate groups—Canada. | LCSH: Mothers and daughters—Canada—Biography. | LCGFT: Autobiographies.
Classification: LCC HN110.Z9 R36 2021 | DDC 320.53—dc23

Cover photo: One Tree Studios www.onetreestudio.ca

Printed in Canada

This book is made of paper from well-managed FSC® - certified forests, recycled materials, and other controlled sources.

For Paul and Nana, Tim and Jan:
thank you for your enduring love and guidance

Authors' Note

Most of the names of those who've passed through our lives before, during and after Lauren's involvement in extremism have been changed to protect privacy. Lauren's late friends Tim and Jan, the staff of Life After Hate, my husband Paul and Paul Fromm are notable exceptions. Each person's memories of this period may differ from ours; this is our memoir and these are our recollections. Our intention is not to vilify or cast blame but rather to show their place within, and impact on, Lauren's journey.

Author's Note

Contents

Introduction   13

Chapter One: A Model Family   19

Chapter Two: He's Gone   32

Chapter Three: Looking for Love   39

Chapter Four: The Recruit   47

Chapter Five: 1488   60

Chapter Six: The Crew   71

Chapter Seven: A New Crew   84

Chapter Eight: Hey, Nazi   100

Chapter Ten: Hammerskins   113

Chapter Eleven: Justice   130

Chapter Twelve: Home. Again.   138

Chapter Thirteen: Intermission   147

Chapter Fourteen: Infiltrating the Mainstream   154

Chapter Fifteen: A Man's World   163

Chapter Sixteen: Tragedy and Clarity   177

Chapter Seventeen: Cutting Ties   185

Chapter Eighteen: The Void   202

Chapter Nineteen: After the Hate   219

Chapter Twenty: In Retrospect   226

Epilogue   233

Acknowledgments   234

Organizations That Can Help   237

Introduction

I didn't set out to raise a skinhead. It just happened.

Okay, it didn't *just* happen. Like most parents, my husband and I had the best of intentions, planning to instill good manners, respect, decency and kindness into both our children. I thought we'd done a fairly good job. But when your last thought before going to sleep is "Will my daughter commit an act of violence against another human being?" you know you've missed something along the way.

There was a time when I worried Lauren—right-wing extremist, skinhead, white supremacist—was capable of violence and racism, the kind that garners front-page headlines, the opening story on the evening news. The sobbing parent crying, "She was a good girl. How could this happen?" could very well have been me.

I knew absolutely nothing about extremism or white supremacy when Lauren first dragged us on this journey. In 2008 I couldn't find articles, groups or forums to help me understand what she was involved in, either in print or online. It wasn't as simple as typing "hate" into a search engine; I really had no clue what I was researching, what keywords to use nor what questions to ask. The police couldn't help either. One constable I contacted told me, "We don't monitor any of the groups operating in and around Toronto."

"Back then, white power groups were probably perceived as a bunch of pissed-off kids," Lauren explains. "Nowadays, it's much worse. Extremists are something to be afraid of." According to Dr. Barbara Perry, the Director of the Centre on Hate, Bias and Extremism, there were approximately one hundred right-wing extremist groups in Canada in 2015; as of 2019 that number had risen to nearly three hundred. Six Canadian groups and/or individuals involved in organized hate, including a one-time Toronto mayoral candidate, were banned from Facebook and Instagram early in 2019, and in June of that year the neo-Nazi group Blood & Honour and its military wing, Combat 18, were added to Canada's terror list. The federal government has partnered with non-profit organizations and other countries to identify and remove hate speech from the internet, chiefly under the guidance of Tech Against Terrorism, a UN-based group supporting the tech industry's battle against extremism. Unfortunately, most white supremacists now blend into the mainstream, their Doc Martens, shaved heads and violent rallies replaced by business suits, professional haircuts and carefully coded content.

What I've learned since Lauren's descent into extremism is that recruiting is often done online. Hate music like National Socialist Black Metal (NSBM), Aryan Black Metal and Neo-Nazi Black Metal offers a potent mixture of anger, aggression and hatred while celebrating violence. Extremists also use video games such as World of Warcraft, various social media platforms and dedicated websites to lure new members. One of the best known is Stormfront, an online blog posting "issues of interest to Canadian White Nationalists" since 1995. Forced to shut down briefly in 2017, it soon resumed its promotion of anti-Semitism, Holocaust denial and Islamaphobia.

Recruiters seek out those who will fall under their spell, targeting kids who are bullied, marginalized or from abusive homes. They'll redirect their rage into racism, then use violence to release the resulting hatred. Tony McAleer, author of *The Cure for Hate: A Former White Supremacist's Journey from Violent Extremism to Radical Compassion* (Arsenal Pulp Press, 2019), maintains that childhood trauma is what drives recruitment, not ideology. Another former recruiter, Christian Picciolini, recounts his own experiences in his book, *White American Youth: My Descent into America's Most Violent Hate Movement—And How I Got Out* (Hachette Books, 2017):

> "It took little skill to spot a teenager with a shitty home life. Somebody without many friends, looking confused or lonely, angry or broke. We would strike up a conversation, find out what they were feeling bad about, and move in with the pitch." (p. 109)

Like alcohol, drug or gambling addiction, hatred is a symptom of a deeper problem, not the problem itself.

But there are positive stories as well. Derek Black, son of the founder of Stormfront and godson of David Duke, the Grand Wizard of the Ku Klux Klan, renounced hate in May 2019 and is now committed to being a catalyst for change. He joins Picciolini, McAleer and others who work to provide the compassion and empathy white power members need to walk away from hate. Life After Hate forums and outreach specialists, including Lauren, support "formers"—people who've left or are leaving extremist groups—and their families. Their website, lifeafterhate.org, features stories of those who've successfully exited white power.

This is the story of Lauren's journey from ordinary kid into the world of hate and white supremacist ideology, but it's also the story of a newly-widowed single parent who had to learn the most difficult lesson of all—how to keep the door open.

Writing this book has been a blessing for our family. Lauren and I, having been brutally honest with one another, are closer than we've ever been and she and her brother now coexist as normal siblings, talking easily without the anger and strain that once dominated our lives. It's our hope that, in sharing our story, parents will recognize parts of it as their own, and will be able to steer their children away from extremism before it's too late.

LAUREN

On August 13, 2017, I was tearing down scaffolding at a residential construction site in Toronto and trading dirty jokes with my coworkers when one of them began talking about the previous day's news story.

"You guys hear what happened in Charlottesville? A white supremacist rammed his car into a group of counter-protesters. What a fucking psychopath, man."

I paused for a second, my head and neck prickling, before replying, "I haven't heard anything about it till now."

"Yeah, there was this white supremacist rally in Virginia and a bunch of counter-protesters showed up yelling, 'This shit isn't cool.' Then a skinhead killed one of the female protesters."

I stayed silent, recalling the life I'd walked away from in 2012. I lead a decent, normal life now. I've been working in construction—scaffolding—for several years, earning enough to own a new pickup truck, and now enjoy friendships with people from all walks of life. Quite a contrast from the life I once led—sporting hate-themed tattoos and Doc Marten boots with telltale white laces, living between the streets and youth shelters, my tough image hiding how miserable I really felt. I'm grateful not to have to face constant judgment for poor decisions I made years before. I'm accepted at face value as the person I am today. No one need know about my past unless I choose to tell them. On rare occasions when I need to prove to myself how far I've come, I can call up my skinhead past, examine it in all its tarnished glory and mentally shove it back into the closet.

Later that night, I was upset to read that thirty-two-year-old Heather Heyer had been killed during the car attack, while others were severely wounded. Twenty-year-old James Alex Fields Jr. had been arrested and charged with murder and malicious wounding. All the while, white supremacists circulated videos of the incident on the internet, defending him or denying his actions altogether.

I'd been living under a rock for the last few years, not paying attention to current events, but I couldn't pretend I was shocked to hear of the Charlottesville tragedy. Back when I'd advocated for the division of humanity, I'd known many lost and angry souls in search of a life purpose. Their discussions had revolved around violence and what they considered cleverly crafted methods of returning society to an all-white population. Back then, I believed them. I was one of them, totally immersing myself in their culture while desensitizing myself to my emotions. I'd taken their ideology as gospel and would have gladly died for it.

Now I see the danger, not only from the hatred of white supremacy but from the backlash against it in communities across the world. What scares me is knowing first-hand that it only takes one individual to ruin the lives of many.

I logged onto Facebook after reading of Heather's death and sure enough, several friends had posted memes encouraging people to "punch Nazis in the face." The most obvious read, "Nazis are bad." Well, no kidding! What I'd submerged myself in *was* bad. But a punch to the face, angry shouts or acts of aggression wouldn't have changed my mind back then. They would have added fuel to my anger.

I wasted five years of my life preaching white power rhetoric, searching for significance at the expense of innocent people. I could make excuses for myself—I never killed or maliciously wounded anyone—but the truth is, I contributed to and influenced events like this. I'd taken part in senseless actions, burying my humanity deep while living a life of hatred.

Once upon a time, I'd helped further the white supremacist movement.

CHAPTER ONE
A Model Family

LAUREN

I grew up in Whitby, Ontario—we called it "White-by"—a mid-sized town on the shore of Lake Ontario. My dad was a police officer with the Toronto Police Service, a Detective Constable who worked in the Youth Bureau, an investigative branch dealing with at-risk youth and sexual assault against children. He was meticulous in gathering evidence, always wanting to bring the bad guys to justice and caring for the victims like they were his own kids.

My mom was fourteen years younger than my dad. He was already thirty-nine when they married and desperately wanted kids. I was born in 1990, two years after their wedding; twenty months later, my brother joined us. My parents always said they felt fortunate to be able to have my mom stay home with us until I was in school. She worked part-time in a clothing store until I was nine, then returned to land surveying, her occupation before I was born.

We spent much of our childhood isolated from the neighbourhood kids, who might have been a bad influence. We followed a strict routine—wake up, go to school, come home, do homework, go to bed—until eventually my parents reluctantly allowed us to go to the park for an hour after school. When I came home five minutes late once, my dad lost his mind. "I thought you'd been kidnapped! Why are you so late?" I tried not to laugh; it never occurred to me his concern stemmed from his work.

I'd always felt off, like I wasn't comfortable in my own skin, but I had several friends in elementary school. In Grade Four, I made friends with Aaron, an awkward, sensitive and slightly goofy boy who was being bullied. As we became closer, our moms started scheduling playdates for us. It felt good to have his friendship, to know I could give him a sense of belonging, and I missed him when I transferred to a new school closer to home at the end of that school year. We didn't reconnect again until high school and, in those intervening years, I'm sure he endured a lot more bullying.

There were many mornings when I'd wake up wanting to be someone else. More than anything, I wanted to make friends, be the cool kid. I noticed that class clowns had the most friends, so I figured getting into trouble would get me there. I got my chance one day when my brother and I had to spend an hour after school at our neighbour's daycare until my mom got home from work. I was twelve and this was another house with rules I didn't want to follow, so I wrote, "shit, fuck, damn and hell" on the chalkboard, then said to the younger kids, "Now, class, today we're going to learn how to spell 'fuck.'" When our neighbour saw what I'd done, she lost it. "Wipe that off the board now," she yelled. I'd gained the attention I'd been looking for.

Music has always been a big part of my life. When I took an interest in the clarinet in elementary school, my parents bought me a used instrument and enrolled me in private lessons so I could learn to play it properly. From grades six to eight I played in the school band. Later I auditioned for and was accepted into the Durham Youth Orchestra and won first place in the Oshawa–Whitby Kiwanis Music Festival, with my grandmother, Nana, playing piano accompaniment.

I loved playing for my uncles, aunts, cousins and grandparents and welcomed their praise, but I also felt pressured to do better. "We want to see you in the Toronto Symphony Orchestra someday," my grandparents would say, their voices filled with too much optimism. The better I did, the more they expected. "You could be doing better," Poppa, my grandfather, would say. At twelve, the pressure seemed to come from everyone around me, and I hoped that being proficient at clarinet would keep me in their good books as my marks at school were up and down.

The summer I turned fourteen, my parents enrolled me in the School of Rock, a week-long camp run through the local college and led by musician Dan Clancy of Lighthouse fame. It was aimed at kids ages ten to fifteen who had an interest in songwriting and playing music.

By then I was tired of playing classical music and wanted to try something different but I knew on that first day that I didn't fit in. Most of the other kids played guitar, bass or drums and dressed the rock 'n' roll bit—ripped jeans, band T-shirts, edgy, dyed hair. I wore track pants and baggy T-shirts, my hair pin-straight and short like a boy's.

Hanna, who already had three years of drum lessons behind her, ate lunch with me that day. She asked if I played anything and, looking anywhere but at her, I said, "I've been playing clarinet for a couple of years."

She laughed. "That isn't going to do you any good here. But good to know."

I was given the choice of learning bass or singing in my assigned band. I couldn't do either, so I chose bass. Our band decided to cover the Blink 182 song, "What's My Age Again?" We practised it for the whole week, until none of us ever wanted to hear it again, so that we could perform it for parents and families on the final day. My dad couldn't get the time off work but my mom came to watch, without my grandparents.

"Why aren't Nana and Poppa here? They come to see me play the clarinet."

"They just don't like this type of music," Mom said.

I didn't believe that was the only reason. I figured it had more to do with me personally, that somehow I'd disappointed them.

The experience at School of Rock made me want to switch from clarinet to bass. My parents agreed, buying me a left-handed Squire Precision bass and enrolling me in private lessons just before the start of my first semester of high school. I hoped to make new friends, maybe even start a band, but none of that happened. The girls at my school were thin and dressed in the latest fashions from stores that didn't cater to my size twelve shape, so I wore baggy boy's cargo pants and over-sized tees. The few pounds I'd gained over the summer had cost me most of my fragile self-esteem; I felt ugly and fat and just wanted to hide. My slipping grades sank even further and I started shutting down emotionally.

That was when I discovered the punk rock and metal scenes. The energy, anger and aggression behind the instrumentals resonated with me and the lyrics assured me that outcasts like me mattered, that I could create my own meaning from their songs. This music became my safe haven. I could put on my headphones and block out whatever was going on in my own head.

The first time I heard Nokturnal Mortum, I'd been randomly googling bands and downloaded one of their songs because I liked their Facebook page. They played NSBM music—National Socialist Black Metal—and their growling lyrics, although hard to understand and not that interesting, drew me in. The darker sound was different from what I'd heard elsewhere. Because it was out of the norm, just like I was, it held a certain fascination. This was definitely not mainstream stuff. Most of the songs spoke of "taking back the land that is rightfully ours" and their loud, aggressive I-want-to-beat-someone-up sound left me feeling almost euphoric. Filled with messages of white unity, the lyrics took second place to the music.

I struggled academically, not being one of those students who could retain information from a book. With every report card, there were phone calls to my parents: "Lauren's doing well in art, music and physical education but . . . " My parents would say to me, "Perhaps you could put as much effort into math and English as you do the fun subjects." It was hard to communicate the reasons behind my struggles, so I started throwing my hands up and saying, "I'm stupid! That's why I'm not doing well in school." They all tried to convince me that wasn't so, but by then I'd allowed so much negative talk into my own head that no one could convince me otherwise.

Things got worse when my grandfather, for whom I'd always been special because I was the first grandchild, began ranting on about higher education. British-born, physically fit, strict and opinionated, Poppa hadn't gone past Grade Ten because of World War II. His elder son had gone to university, my mom had gone to college to study architectural drafting and her other brother had "made something of himself" without any post-secondary education. Yet when I said I thought I'd like to go to college instead of university, his reply was, "You're nothing if you don't go to university."

I had already failed to meet his musical and academic expectations; sports was another disappointment. The year I turned fourteen, in addition to switching from clarinet to bass, I switched from soccer to baseball. Poppa had paid for and attended every single soccer game, as it was his favourite sport, but he wanted nothing to do with baseball. I felt like he'd tossed me aside, like I'd done something wrong. Then he began shaming me for carrying a bit more weight than most other girls my age: "You're not going to get a boyfriend if you look like that" and "We should keep the food away from you." My appearance and ability to get a boyfriend seemed to be all that mattered.

Poppa disliked all visible minorities, Jews and gays, and had no problem sharing his views with my brother and me. As I got older, I realized I didn't dare come forward with my own secret—that I was confused about my own sexuality. It didn't matter what my parents said afterwards, how they tried to downplay his remarks, his repeated rejection of gays made me feel angry and completely alone.

My ideas didn't seem to matter. I once told him Goth kids were good people and that some of my friends dressed that way just to express themselves. His response was, "No, they aren't good people. They're a bad influence on you." In spite of what my parents said— "Ignore him. He's a bitter old man who'll never change"—it pissed me off. It was like I had no voice.

That same year my mother's family was suddenly torn apart by jealousy and bitterness. I didn't understand much of it but, when Poppa shut all of us out, I felt I was somehow to blame. I was confused and hurt. Nana, a quiet lady who shared my love of music and crafts, visited when she could but that's when it really sunk in that I was no longer someone my grandfather cared about—I'd failed academically, musically, athletically and socially. Family is supposed to love you unconditionally, but suddenly that was not the case.

JEANETTE

I can't count the times I wished for the help of Mary Poppins. During those first weeks at home with my newborn daughter, I struggled to fall in love with her, to feel that rush of emotion portrayed in TV commercials and soap operas. What kind of mother had to work to feel that way about her child? I asked myself constantly. One who was overwhelmed and unsure of herself, that's who. When Lauren was about six weeks old, I called my mother in tears. "She won't stop crying. I'm going to kill her!"

She laughed softly and said, "Put her in her crib for five minutes. Let her cry. And go make yourself a cup of tea."

Sure enough, Lauren settled down and so did I. Shortly afterwards, I experienced that golden moment—I reached into her crib, her shining eyes laughed up at me and I fell head over heels. That was one of the best moments of my life.

My parents were almost as ecstatic at Lauren's birth as her father and

I were. Other than Paul, who proudly carried her around the hospital corridors for the first forty-five minutes of her life, they were the first to see her, to hold her, to bond with her. Living only twenty minutes away, they were the first to volunteer for babysitting or to drop around for a cup of tea. My mom knitted dozens of sweaters, hats and mittens, sewed quilts and crocheted blankets and crib afghans for both kids, while my father, a carpenter by trade, built rocking horses, a cradle and slider chairs for Lauren and her brother. Lauren was the first grandchild, and her brother the only grandson.

Our kids were far down the chain of succession in Paul's family, being eighth and ninth out of twelve grandchildren. His parents were lovely, very gracious towards me and excited when we told them we were expecting, but when Lauren was born they visited for only a short time so my parents could spend time with their first grandchild. I'd hoped they'd come more often as the months wore on but there always seemed to be another grandchild who needed their attention. Paul's mom once said to me, "Your mother does such beautiful knitted work. Mine could never be that good." Try as I might, I couldn't convince her that what was important to us was the love behind the gifts. Eventually, I began to see why Paul kept his family at a distance. As the eldest of six, his mother had leaned on him until he left home in his late teens. He'd always felt responsible for his siblings and his role as adviser and problem-solver inhibited rather than encouraged closeness.

I have a photo of twenty-month-old Lauren, wearing yellow footie pajamas, seated beside her dad on the couch, sharing his chocolate ice cream. I loved watching their routine—one spoonful for dad, one for Lauren—waiting for Paul to double-dip, the gleam of laughter lighting his eyes when Lauren realized she'd been duped. Her knowing look, as if she were aware of his scheme the whole time, speaks volumes about the intelligence she possessed, without hinting at the darker side that would later emerge.

As the children grew, Paul and I began referring to them as "the twins." They were of similar height, were interested in the same toys and TV shows and, when together, behaved as if they were twins. For months we'd sail along in our bubble of joy. Then Lauren would become defiant, challenging and difficult, throwing tantrums and taking advantage of her brother.

"What if I took away your favourite toy? How would you feel?" I'd ask.

"You can't take my toy!"

When a friend was introduced into the mix, Lauren often treated her brother badly, playing only with the friend or outright ignoring him. She seemed to lack the ability to share his feelings, his sadness or hurt, her reply always combative, always about her. Having been spanked as a child, I knew how wrong it was but when Lauren really challenged me, I have to admit I resorted to a few carefully placed smacks on her bum.

Paul laughingly referred to me as the General because, due to his work shifts, I was the primary disciplinarian. He would scold the children on occasion but, because he and Lauren had a wonderfully strong bond, he'd go a little softer on her than I would. I'm sure he felt I was softer on our son for the same reason.

When Lauren was in Grade One, the school offered a parenting course, which I eagerly took part in. At that point, I'd run out of ways to discipline her. She didn't watch much TV so taking it away wasn't a punishment. Yelling or trying to reason with her didn't work—she'd just throw a tantrum. So, when they showed us how to use time-outs, I thought I'd found the holy grail. The only problem was Lauren liked being in her room, so I had to find a place where I could watch her and still have it seem like a punishment.

We were strict parents who tried to instill good manners in our kids, expecting them to be polite to other kids and adults alike, share toys with each other and behave when out in public. One of my admonitions was, "If you're going to misbehave, make sure it's at home. No temper tantrums in stores, no bad behaviour at friends' houses."

I was mortified when my neighbour told me what Lauren had said and done in front of her daycare kids. We thought it was a bonus not to have to put the children into regular daycare where they might pick up bad habits; we wanted our kids to be people we liked, people we wanted to spend time with, not the mouthy, over-indulged brats we'd run into at the park or mall. Now it was my child who'd misbehaved. "I'm ashamed to have to face our neighbours now. Do you realize how difficult you've made things for us? How am I going to find suitable after-school care if she lets us go?" I could not get Lauren to admit she'd done it. She claimed I was siding with them, that she was the victim, that one of the boys had written those words on the board and blamed her.

I knew from Lauren's defensiveness that she was lying, but I was stuck between what I knew and what I could prove, as I had been with the countless incidents that had come before. Lauren had perfected her ability to lie, along with an outstanding talent for exaggeration and an it-doesn't-matter attitude, in elementary school. I would arrive to see her standing off by herself her, face carefully blank, watching the other kids run around her like she wasn't even there. A visit to her Grade Two class had alerted me to a teacher who barely acknowledged Lauren's presence and the favouritism shown to the popular kids whose parents were the cool ones. It didn't seem to matter how often I volunteered for class trips or craft days—my child was destined to be an outsider because I wasn't one of the "it" parents, the well-dressed moms who gave extravagant gifts at Christmas and year's end, the beautiful ones who chatted easily with teachers about things other than their kids. My heart broke for her.

I often had to remind myself—and Lauren—that while I might not like her behaviour, I still loved her. I'd had a lifetime to learn the difference and wasn't going to let my children grow up feeling unloved, as I had. My own father hadn't been what I needed and there was no way I was going to parent his way. I knew how deeply it hurt to think your parent, the one person who was supposed to love you no matter what, didn't give a damn about you, or worse, wished you'd never been born.

In my family, my father's rules were law. He made it clear he hadn't wanted me when I was four years old and playfully hid in my closet when he came to say goodbye. Rather than gamely looking for me, he muttered something under his breath and walked out and, from then on, ignored me, looking through me as if I weren't even there. I was the only one of his three children to consistently challenge him, which seemed to give him further licence to treat me with contempt. He put conditions on his family and friends—more than one of his buddies had been cut from his life after disagreeing with him—and I endured many years of his silent treatments. In fact, I'd failed to meet every one of my father's standards, except for providing him with grandchildren.

Music was a big part of our family life. Lauren's dad would play the oldies at home or in the car; my own car was stuffed with CDs and cassette tapes, both mine and those Lauren and her brother enjoyed. Music, for both my kids, provided the same cushion for life's triumphs and tragedies as it had for me—Leo Sayer and Air Supply for broken hearts, Streetheart and AC/DC blasting from car speakers on a Friday night cruise through Oshawa, and Queen's "Bohemian Rhapsody," which said everything I'd felt as a gawky teen.

We were thrilled when Lauren asked for a clarinet, excited as she went from learning notes to playing songs, and happy to have her play for my parents and our families. The Youth Orchestra was a way to introduce her to the importance of playing with others and the Kiwanis Festival was a chance for her to play in front of an audience, to show how far she'd come. We were proud of her but didn't push, making sure to tell her, "When you stop enjoying it, we'll stop the lessons."

I saw Rock Camp as an opportunity for Lauren to be with kids her own age, to see how music was made and how much work went into her favourite songs. I'd hoped she'd fit in, that the kids would be less preppy than her schoolmates and more accepting. Her dad and I were proud of her for trying something new but I quickly realized she felt like an outsider. We happily agreed to buy her a used bass and lessons afterwards, but nothing could lessen her disappointment when her grandparents failed to show for the final performance. I tried to explain that they had very little patience for anything they didn't like, but Lauren wouldn't accept that it wasn't somehow her fault. She began pulling further into her shell, worrying me more.

From the outside, we were a model family. Behind the scenes, my father peppered us, as he had my entire life, with his opinions and prejudices, freely sharing his intense dislike for Blacks, "Pakis" and immigrants, despite the fact that he himself had emigrated from England in 1954, leaving behind a sister who'd married a Black man and borne four mixed-race children. We'd hear how "goddamned Blacks should go back where they came from" and "immigrants come here wanting handouts. Nobody gave me handouts when I came over."

"How can he hate Blacks but enjoy drinking with Uncle Roy?" I asked my mom time and again.

I had learned at an early age to keep my opinions to myself, and neither Paul nor I challenged him directly out of respect. Instead, we tried to reinforce *our* opinions, *our* views and *our* rules as the only ones Lauren and her brother should pay attention to. After every visit to my parents' house, we'd talk to the kids about what had been said. Then we'd debrief and reassure them they didn't have to do as Poppa wanted. They could do anything, be anything they wanted to be, our love for them wouldn't change.

"Poppa said I have to go to university," Lauren would say.

"Poppa wants everyone to make him look good by doing what he tells them," I'd reply. "You do what you want. If you want to work, that's fine. If you want to go to college, that's good too. As long as you're happy with your life, that's all that matters. It's not up to you to make Poppa happy."

The family split had nothing to do with Lauren. I offered to coordinate a family photo session to celebrate my parents' fiftieth anniversary. My oldest brother, who'd earned a master's degree and whose career had taken him into the hallowed halls of the Ontario government, and his equally accomplished wife, already past child-bearing age when they married, were jealous of the perceived attention we received because we had produced the grandchildren. (My other brother and his wife had two girls but they lived on the west coast and were consequently not as involved.) My sister-in-law believed I was prohibiting their dog from being included in the photo; she sent my mother a letter saying so and listing a number of other grievances. My father decided to side with his son and cut us from his life. Suddenly my children, my husband and I were *persona non grata* at my parents' house. I was hurt that my mother hadn't stood up for me, but she was a loving, quiet, subservient woman who, having been raised by a strict mother who'd treated her as a house-maid, wasn't practised in giving voice to her own opinions. She didn't want to lose either of her children, couldn't deal with the sudden onslaught of malice erupting from all sides and, sadly, had no power to change my father's mind.

Once I worked through the emotional side of things with a great therapist, I was able to see the favour my brother had done us. Perhaps it was too late, but at last Lauren and her brother were free of the stranglehold my father had placed on them. Instead, we were free to enjoy my mom's love, laugh at her crazy sense of humour and experience the profound enjoyment she felt when she was with us. Always my go-to person when Paul wasn't home and parenting didn't go according to plan, it was a joy to see her blossom while interacting with her grandchildren, to watch my kids grow in her love.

The other cloud over our family life, one that we didn't share with the children, was Paul's myelodysplasia, which was diagnosed when Lauren was only seven. For years he'd blamed being tired on shift work but after his mother's death in 1997 he had a complete physical. We were both shocked to find out he had an incurable illness that could lead to leukemia and shorten his lifespan.

CHAPTER TWO

He's Gone

LAUREN _____

I was sixteen when my dad was diagnosed with acute myeloid leukemia in 2006. He'd retired from the police force in July and by
mid-August he'd been admitted to Princess Margaret Hospital in
Toronto for chemotherapy and a possible stem cell transplant. The
day we took him to the hospital, he had to wait hours to be admitted.
He was really nervous, angry and upset, far from the confident man I
knew. I'd only seen him like that a few times and I didn't know what
to say or do. I felt lost and helpless.

I'd always put his lack of energy down to age and was angry that
my parents, wanting to protect us, hadn't told us anything about his
illness. Everything was happening quickly, but I still believed him
when he said he'd live for years to come. "I want to do chemo so I'll
have the chance to be around longer for you guys."

For the next five months, we drove an hour into the city to visit
him. At first, we'd go every other day, but when September hit we
could only go on Saturdays. Gramps and one of my uncles visited
him every Sunday and his other siblings went when they could so
between them, us and his work friends, he had visitors almost every
day. It was weird not having him at home. He'd been larger than
life and my best friend, always around, always encouraging. He had
always taken a special interest in my woodworking class, enthusing
about everything I'd made. "Wow, look at this," he'd say, as he marvelled at the smallest details. "Your sanding job is always so clean."

The medical team didn't begin chemo right away so he didn't look much different on our first few visits, but once they began wiping out his old bone marrow to prepare him for the transplanting of healthy stem cells—two of his brothers were matches—he changed. His face thinned out as he lost weight, the drugs altering his body and short-term memory. He'd always been the person who could fill a room just by standing in the doorway; within two months, he looked like a skeleton, his sagging flesh hanging off bones clearly visible beneath his hospital gown.

But he was still our dad. When a nurse had shaved his head, telling him, "You'll lose what precious little hair you have anyway," he was surprisingly happy with his new look, comparing himself to Mark Messier, the hockey player. I could no longer tease him with "Comb-over," the nickname I'd given him years before. I have a vivid memory of him trying to convince my shy, quiet brother to talk to a girl he liked. "Why don't you just go talk to her?" Because my brother was nothing like my dad, I found this funny. But late that fall, when my dad's heart rate went through the roof and he was transferred to the ICU, I began to get scared. Once they'd stabilized him after a week or so of close monitoring, he became quite docile, which was not like him.

In early December, my brother, mother and I, along with Gramps and two of my uncles, met with some of my dad's doctors in a hospital boardroom. My mom had asked my dad's family to be there for support but also because she figured they should hear what had happened. My dad had fallen into a coma. The doctors used medical terms I didn't understand, but basically they said his chances of coming out of the coma were slim and that his quality of life would suck if he ever regained consciousness. The chemo had damaged his heart and most of his organs—his personality, his physical self and basic bodily functions would no longer be what they'd been four months before. None of us could picture my dad as anyone other than who'd he'd always been—strong, capable and in charge—and the doctors encouraged my mom to sign a Do Not Resuscitate order.

The last time I saw my dad was on a Saturday night in January, just hours before he died. We were standing around watching him sleep and I thought his breathing sounded odd, like he was double inhaling. But I was still sure he'd pull through because he'd always been so strong and stubborn.

The phone rang at 11:30 that night. My mom told my brother and me that the doctor had given my dad less than twenty-four hours to live, that she was heading to the hospital. I wanted to go with her—I knew I'd regret it if I didn't. My brother stayed home, saying, "I want to remember him the way he was." After Nana arrived to keep him company, Mom and I drove into the city. My mind was going in all directions—the doctors had been wrong before so maybe they'd be wrong again. But when my mom hit the steering wheel and cried out, "He and I were supposed to be growing old together. This isn't supposed to happen," I got really scared.

When the elevator doors opened, the doctor was waiting by my dad's room. "He's gone," he said quietly and ushered us inside.

What do you mean, he's gone? I wanted to say. I sat on the windowsill watching my mom hold his hand and kiss his face. I'd known something was wrong when we were there earlier, but it took some time for me to believe he was dead. There was a deep, black void inside me as we gathered all his stuff and took it out to the car. The next day seemed surreal, like a nightmare. Mom got tons of calls so I couldn't use the phone to call Aaron, with whom I'd reconnected, nor my newest friend, Austin, an autistic kid in my class who I'd been hanging around with most of the summer. I was lonely, trying to come to grips with losing my father, and suddenly I had too much time on my hands.

The funeral was packed with family, friends and coworkers. They even opened a second room with TV monitors because there were so many people there. I felt both comforted and overwhelmed by the huge turnout, but I'd never met most of them and most of them didn't know who I was either. My dad lay inside the coffin, wearing his favourite suit and the makeup the funeral home had put on him. He didn't look like himself.

Dad's former partner, his old boss, younger sister and brother and my mom's brother (the one we were still in touch with) all spoke, their tributes full of funny stories that somehow made us laugh and cry at the same time. A new friend from a nearby bible chapel, who'd gotten to know dad while he was in hospital, gave a great eulogy. Every story highlighted a different piece of my dad's life, but in the end everyone said the same thing—he was a caring man, willing to do anything to help others. I was proud of my dad, proud of what each person said about him. But I knew that none of it was going to bring him back.

JEANETTE

By the time Lauren hit Grade Eleven, our family life had changed dramatically. My husband, after living with myelodysplasia for nearly ten years, was diagnosed with leukemia that August and entered hospital less than a week later.

I kept a diary from the first day of Paul's diagnosis, a running commentary on his medical care and treatments, as well as personal observations on his mental and physical state. It served to help me be his voice, his advocate as a myriad of doctors and nurses rotated through his room.

His first two weeks went well, the IV hydrating him so he looked better than he had for months, even though his Hickman line would eventually cause him distress. Twelve days in, he began receiving chemo; three days later, its effects started to show as he developed mouth sores, lesions, swollen feet and itchy skin. Fifteen days later he'd gained twenty pounds of fluid, seemingly overnight, and was finding it increasingly hard to stay positive. And when the doctors admitted him to the intensive care unit of Mount Sinai Hospital three days after, it became apparent that Paul was in for a rough ride. Through countless ups and downs—accelerated heart rate, fevers and shakes, low blood pressure and difficulties breathing—I monitored his vitals, asked questions and relayed messages to family and friends.

Two months after entering hospital, Paul became depressed, admitting he was tired of the whole thing. December first brought a sudden emergency meeting between the doctors, me, the kids and Paul's family. "Your husband is on life support," they said baldly. "A tube is breathing for him, his blood pressure is being controlled by drugs, the heart valve has been badly damaged and the fungal infection (one he'd been fighting since the Hickman line's insertion) has spread to his organs and brain. We'll reassess him in a week, if he doesn't go into cardiac arrest before then."

Paul was comatose for three days, and when he eventually awoke I continued to believe in him, in his strength of will, his conviction to live. I was his voice, grilling the doctors about medications, each procedure, every small change in my husband's health and demeanour. His mental state varied, hallucinations giving way to depression and anger, as he barked out orders for me to follow. Christmas was a sad, difficult day, the kids opening their dad's gifts at his bedside until he tired of their chatter. New Year's Day brought more pain as Paul confessed, "I don't think I'm going to live much longer," even though his blood counts were improving.

As Paul grew weaker, I had to grow stronger. Yet, when I was once again called to discuss his situation with the primary oncologist, I refused to hear what she was really telling me. "He's addicted to the pain meds. We're going to scale them back a little, giving him enough to keep him pain-free but allowing him to be more lucid, more with it. And we've decided that, should he have another cardiac incident, we will not move him from his room here at Princess Margaret to the ICU at Mount Sinai." I couldn't accept that what she was really saying was, "We're going to keep him here, keep him comfortable. Until he dies."

That Saturday night, when the phone rang and the doctor said, "I'm sorry. We don't expect Paul to live past the next twenty-four hours," I understood how it felt to have one's heart break. His face was still warm when Lauren and I arrived at his bedside. I kissed him for the last time and then stumbled numbly around his room, collecting five months' worth of personal supplies, cards, gifts and clothing before driving home in shocked silence. Lauren went straight to her room while I sat and cried on my mother's shoulder until the wee hours of Sunday morning.

The phone calls, preparations and arrangements kept me from feeling the full weight of grief during the days between Paul's death and funeral. My second brother, living out west by then, flew in and sat in front with me, my mom and the kids. My father, whose only words to me were, "I'm sorry," along with my oldest brother and his wife, who hugged me with false assurances of "you know we love you," sat several rows behind. During the service, we were blessed by the outpouring of friends and family who shared our love and loss. We laughed and cried through each wonderful eulogy, secure in the notion that everyone present knew how special Paul was.

Once the service and luncheon were over, my mom, who had been our rock through everything, caved in to my father's demands. "I'm so sorry. I feel as though I'm letting you down, but everyone is going back to our house and they're expecting me to make them dinner," she said through tears. "I'll call you later." Bereft of her support, I asked Paul's father and siblings back to our house for coffee, desperate to stave off the inevitable loneliness and pain I knew we'd all feel. "We're all going back to dad's," one of his brothers told me. "We figured we'd be in the way at your place." None of Paul's family knew of our estrangement from my family. "I'll call you tomorrow," he said with a brief hug.

Abandoned by those we needed most, the three of us went home to an empty house, each sequestering in the privacy of our own rooms. Later that night, as they shouted and argued over something trivial, I saw how much my children's grief overwhelmed them. When both families walked away from me hours after burying Paul, they also walked away from Lauren and her brother.

CHAPTER THREE

Looking for Love

LAUREN_____

A few months after my dad's passing in January 2007, my school gave a crisis presentation on self-harming. Rather than hearing a warning call, I learned about something that could provide me with the relief I craved. I began cutting myself, usually with razor blades, and soon became addicted to the release of endorphins that came with it. I didn't do it all the time. Days would go by without me needing it but then something—loneliness, a memory of my dad, an argument with my mom—would create the urge to *feel* something again. Cutting was easy to turn to and became the crutch I relied on to get through the school year.

My friendship with Austin hadn't survived my dad's death, and Aaron and I were drifting apart. I was desperate to be someone else and traded my tomboy look for a more girly one. Wearing makeup didn't help, so one day I struck up a conversation with Drew, a guy I knew from Grade Ten English. He and his friends were social outcasts, like me, and I knew from their band shirts that they liked metal music. Also like me, they disliked how the preppy jocks treated girls like objects. I found them respectful and, for the first time in a long time, felt like I had real friends. Pretty soon, we were getting alcohol twice a week from one of their older siblings, drinking it after classes and on weekends in the wooded area behind the school.

The need to self-harm dissipated that summer as I continued drinking with the metalhead guys in between trying to finish my Community Involvement volunteer hours, something I had to do for school credit but hadn't finished during the school year. I couldn't see the point to life when I was sober but felt happier when drinking. I decided that the real me was the one who loved being wild. I became the black-out drunk who did stupid things—running naked across the park—and never remembered what she'd done. I'd sneak out at night, wait until I could walk straight before going home and then drink lots of water before bed. Luckily, my mom never caught me drunk and I never suffered from hangovers.

When I wasn't out drinking or volunteering, I was spending time with my father's family, something my mom kept pushing. I'd stayed in touch with my two cousins on my mom's side, Charlee and Victoria, through MSN Instant Messenger after they'd moved west, so I didn't hesitate to give my email address to my cousin Regina when she asked. At first, we shared harmless conversation, venting about school; she'd dropped out for a time and I was still there, hating every minute of it. But when I complained of being an outcast, I could tell she couldn't relate—everyone on that side of the family was attractive, confident, sociable and popular.

It was nice having a female peer, even though Regina was a bit overpowering. When we visited her family, she'd sometimes act like my best friend, but soon after she would tear me down again, bossing me around, which made me feel bad about myself. I knew I was expected to follow her around everywhere. Once she commanded me to "come" when she went outside for a smoke; I went along so my mom wouldn't bitch at me. Eventually she encouraged me to stop wearing makeup and to dye my hair blond, something I couldn't imagine would look remotely attractive.

Still, I envied her because she had a large social circle. I hung out with her and her friends a couple of times, but I thought many of her friends' conversations were petty and shallow. They reminded me of the school kids I didn't like. I began to realize being cool wasn't all it was cracked up to be and wasn't really worth the accompanying drama. But I went along with it all until school started again and we didn't have to see each other as often.

At the beginning of the fall semester, I made arrangements to meet up with Jay, a guy who'd messaged me in the summer: *Hey, we're in the same Facebook group for metal.* He told me he was a twenty-four-year-old metalhead who worked full-time at General Motors in Oshawa. With music in common, we'd chatted for a few months before I accidentally told my mother, who instantly assumed he would turn out to be a stalker or murderer.

"You don't know this guy," she pointed out. "He could be some old guy sitting behind his computer luring young girls. Some pathetic loser who's playing games with you."

"You're just saying that because you don't want me to have any friends."

"Have you actually met him in person?"

"Why are you always suspicious about everyone? He's really nice. He cares about me, unlike you."

I snuck out of the house the evening we were supposed to meet but he didn't show up. I waited an hour and then walked home, realizing my mom was probably right—he was a dickhead just playing games. Not that I was ready to admit it.

In November I began dating my first real boyfriend. Connor was a classmate of Greek heritage, tall and skinny, with brown hair, who asked me if I wanted to date him after we kissed at a party. I said I'd give it a try and then overheard him saying that he was going out with me because he wanted to look good in front of his ex. It hurt knowing I was being used but I was just happy that someone liked me. I didn't like myself and had been afraid that no one else would either.

JEANETTE

I found out the hard way that everyone grieves differently. Lauren had never been one to cry or show emotion other than anger, so it was difficult for me to perceive her feelings. She wouldn't talk about her father and wouldn't listen to me unless I said something she agreed with, routinely exhibiting her stony-faced, I-don't-give-a-shit attitude.

There were more than a few hints of Lauren's growing anger—her unwillingness to listen or compromise, barely checked temper, penchant for throwing whatever object was closest at hand and her constant slamming of doors—but I truly believed that her brother, grandmother, extended family, friends and I could provide whatever she was searching for, whatever she needed. That we could be her support system, helping her navigate the grief and sadness she couldn't express and wouldn't deal with.

My son, in many ways similar to his sister, retreated into himself, often spending hours in his room, alone with his grief. Always a good student, he poured himself into his schoolwork, burying his emotions as if doing so would vanquish them completely. His dad had passed away at the start of school exams, but rather than accepting grades he'd already earned, something the principal had suggested, he insisted on not only taking the exams but not telling his teachers or friends about his dad's death. He refused to cry—at least in front of me—and seldom spoke of his father, holding in all his pain, anguish, anger and loneliness.

I was working full-time to keep a roof over our heads, trying desperately to be both father and mother, blaming myself for Paul's death—rehashing every telltale sign I must have missed that would have led to an earlier diagnosis—while mourning him. Exhausted both physically and emotionally, I tried to help both kids through Paul's passing by keeping his spirit alive. On my son's birthday, just weeks after his dad's death, I gave him and Lauren framed photos of themselves with Paul, thinking they'd be nice reminders. I talked about him every day and displayed pictures of better times until, about two months after his funeral, Lauren yelled, "I don't want to talk about Dad again!"

Undeterred, I continued with plans for Lauren, her brother and me to see Paul's family, to keep his memory alive that way. Big family dinners at Gramps' had always involved a lot of commotion and Paul's huge personal presence usually guaranteed he'd be the one steering conversations, the rest of us comfortable in his shadow. Now, without him there, the three of us felt like strangers. We struggled to feel comfortable and I persevered, assuming it would benefit all of us to maintain a relationship. I think I also wanted to belong to them myself in a way I no longer belonged in my own family.

I'd hoped that Lauren and Regina, relatively close in age, could become closer but although Regina had the best of intentions, offering support and friendship, I could see the two girls were worlds apart. Lauren had never felt at ease with the pretty girls at school and viewed Regina's overtures with suspicion.

"She's trying," I said to Lauren more than once. "You need to meet her halfway."

"She's trying to make me into herself," Lauren argued. "I'm just a project for her."

"Okay, maybe she's going about it wrong but at least she's trying to include you."

In the end, it seemed there could be no middle ground for two teenaged girls from opposite ends of the spectrum. One oozed confidence, had a large group of friends and came from a loving two-parent home while the other preferred to stay in the shadows, befriended strays and had lost the one parent she'd always adored. They had nothing in common but blood.

Early into the spring semester, I explained to both kids that there weren't enough hours in the day for me to supervise homework the way their father had. He had been the very definition of a helicopter parent, sitting with Lauren for hours while she completed assignments. I'd be there to help if needed but it would be their responsibility to do their homework themselves. Instead of taking me up on my offer, Lauren lied to me. Her interim report card that spring showed a grade of fifty percent in math and biology, and both teachers commented on her lack of motivation. "Those classes are boring," she said, "and my teachers are mean." As the school year wound down, I had a call from Lauren's math teacher. "She's in danger of failing," he said.

Family life became one of isolation punctuated with arguments. By the time I got home from work, Lauren would be in her room. At dinner she'd rarely say a word and, once done, she'd head back upstairs to spend the rest of the night by herself. I was relieved that I didn't have to deal with her moods, tantrums and nasty comments. My son also preferred his own company and, as my arguments with Lauren increased, I saw less and less of him.

Things came to a head on Mother's Day, when Lauren and I began arguing over something trivial. The more I tried to reason with her, the less she listened and the nastier she became until she finally screamed, "Fuck you!"

"Well, Happy Mother's Day to me," I muttered as I pushed her out of my room, slammed the door and sank to my bed with a box of tissues, preparing for yet another pity party. What the hell did I do to deserve this? I asked myself. I'd done the best I could for my kids, taking over everything Paul had once looked after—paying bills, household maintenance, banking—as well as finalizing his estate and keeping things exactly as they'd been before his death. No new school. No moving to a smaller house or rental apartment. No financial burdens to challenge my kids' futures. Try as I might, I couldn't shake the hurt and anger Lauren provoked in me.

I took both kids to my therapist to find a middle ground where we could communicate without shouting or ignoring each other. The three of us sat together uncomfortably as I explained what had been happening. The therapist then asked both kids how they felt about Paul's passing, how I'd been handling it, what they'd each like to see change and what bothered them most. The hardest part for me was accepting their desire to hear "less of Dad" from me. That stung. I felt they were pushing his memory from their lives, not realizing how painful it was for them just hearing his name. When she explained we were all mourning in different ways, I agreed to talk about him only when they spoke of him first. I also promised to try to keep my temper when situations began to escalate, counting to ten before speaking or leaving the room until I felt in control. She asked Lauren to take responsibility for her name-calling, swearing and lack of empathy.

For a while, it seemed to work. Then I found Lauren sitting on the floor one night, her back to the bed, a razor blade poised above her arm. Angry welts and red scars stood out in sharp relief on her beautiful pale skin. I cried, my voice shaking as I asked, "Why are you doing this?" Taking the blade from her, I hoped that by talking, opening up, I might convince her to stop. But even though she teared up and allowed me to keep the blade, I knew that somehow, somewhere along the line, I'd lost her love, her confidence and her respect.

This wasn't normal behaviour. I was certain she hadn't come up with this idea on her own but, alone in this painful, uncharted territory, I didn't feel able to confide in family or friends, fearing they'd think the worst of us, that they'd see how flawed we were as people, as a family. Instead, I called the high school's vice-principal the following morning, reasoning she'd probably witnessed her share of teenage angst and would be bound by confidentiality not to spill our secrets. She agreed to meet me to talk about the cutting and explained, "Lauren's not trying to hurt herself. It's not about suicide. It's about controlling the pain, releasing it in whatever way she can."

On Canada Day 2007, the kids and I took off on a road trip to Ottawa and through to the east coast. For eleven blissful days, we laughed, talked and lived as if we hadn't just experienced the worst loss possible. The scenery was lovely, the people friendly and our three days on Prince Edward Island filled with great times and open discussions about Paul and his passing. I wanted to harness that period of our lives, to bottle such happiness, however brief, for what I knew would be hard times to come.

When we returned home, Lauren and I began bickering on and off about her getting a part-time job. I'd worked from the time I turned sixteen and expected my kids to do the same, so the fact that she refused to even consider it really upset me. As far as I knew, Lauren spent most of the summer in her room. As both kids had always been homebodies, I'd never had to set a curfew and, exhausted by day's end, was unaware if they left the house at night.

At the start of Lauren's final year of high school, she let slip that she'd been chatting with someone named Jay. I'd warned both kids to be careful online, but apparently only one of them had listened. I tried discussing the perils of her behaviour, gave examples of real-life situations with bad endings, but Lauren wrote them off as hysteria. As far as she was concerned, I was overreacting, blowing things way out of proportion.

I was furious when my son told me she'd gone to meet this Jay in a parking lot a mile or so east of us, late at night. Lauren didn't see this guy for who he was—a user, a scumbag who was toying with her. And while I never said, "I told you so," I was hoping my daughter would see that I understood the outside world slightly better than she did.

Lauren told me a bit about Connor and I wasn't too impressed at first, but he seemed nice enough when he was at our place. She brought a few of her guy friends by too, all really nice, down-to-earth kids who seemed respectful and decent, none of them drinking or swearing while I was within earshot. After spending so much time isolated in her room, I was pleased that she had a boyfriend and some friends to hang out with. I hoped her girlfriend status, along with a new peer group, would help boost her self-confidence. Maybe, I thought, the worst was over.

CHAPTER FOUR

The Recruit

LAUREN_____

In early November 2007, I was on Nokturnal Mortum's Facebook page when I received a message from a guy named Donny: *I was wondering if you're NS or just listening to NSBM?*

I didn't know what he meant. Figuring NS and NSBM were music genres, I responded, *I'm not NS, I just listen to the music.*

When I asked what he listened to, he supplied me with a list of other NSBM bands, asking, *What else do you like?*

I gave him my list, not realizing that some of it, at least according to Donny, leaned towards racism. *With all of this you must lean to the NS side of things.*

I had a hard time understanding a lot of NSBM lyrics, mostly because the recording quality was so bad, but not wanting to sound stupid, I didn't ask what NS meant. I just enjoyed having someone to talk to.

A few days later, Donny messaged me that his friend in Ottawa had been beaten up by a couple of Black guys: *This is how us white people get treated. And Blacks get away with this shit.*

I wasn't exactly sure what Donny meant but it sounded a lot like what Poppa used to say. It was familiar, which made me think it must be true. I didn't know how to respond so I changed the subject, writing about the preppy kids at school I couldn't stand. When Donny called them "a bunch of mainstream sheep" I had to laugh, the label fit so well. We continued messaging every few days and, two weeks after our first conversation, Donny suggested we meet up. I wanted to know him a bit better first, so I said I'd call him instead. The first time we spoke on the phone, he seemed more interested in yelling at his neighbour, which made me laugh, especially with his Scottish lilt. During our third conversation he told me, "Jewish people are very elitist. If you think the people at your school are preps, you should meet some Jews. They're exclusive, a real chore to be around. They look down their noses at you." I'd never known anyone who was Jewish but reasoned that he probably knew more about people than I did. After all, he was twenty-six and lived in the city.

For the next few weeks, I dated Connor, listened to metal and NSBM, downloaded more bands like Nokturnal Mortum and talked to Donny, who said nothing more about whites, Jews or Blacks. I liked the way he spoke to me, as though he'd known me forever. He told me, "You're smarter than everyone else around you. There need to be more girls in the world like you." He made me feel like I mattered.

Sometime around the beginning of December, Donny finally labelled his way of thinking as National Socialism and began referring to "the movement." He explained that Jews controlled the world and that Blacks were trying to get back at white people for enslaving them. History books were trying to instill a sense of shame and guilt in white kids, just for being white. He was part of a resistance movement fighting to ensure the white population survived. The movement included individual groups called crews that could be identified by common symbols: white laces in Doc Martens boots, specific tattoos and coded language. Some crews also had their own symbols, fabric patches embroidered with swastikas, Celtic crosses or slogans that were earned and worn to show personal commitment.

Donny told me about Stormfront—a white supremacist, white nationalist, anti-Semitic, neo-Nazi internet forum—and I created an account, 'educating' myself every day about how liberal whites were being brainwashed. Donny referred to everyone outside the movement as sheep, telling me it was good to be different, so this new knowledge made me feel better than they were. I kept reading so I could throw the movement's rhetoric at anyone who challenged me.

I was learning to fear and resent anyone whose skin wasn't white but was having a harder time accepting Donny's views on gays and lesbians. I was afraid my turmoil, my secret, would come out. Even though I'd talked openly with my parents about sex, we'd usually discussed being gay or straight, never bisexual; I hadn't known you could be attracted to both males and females. I couldn't talk to Donny and wouldn't talk to my mom, so I repressed my feelings and ignored my doubts—I'd already invested a lot of time into white power and didn't want to find out it was all for nothing.

Whenever we talked, Donny would use whatever I said to lead the conversation into his own narrative about the victimization of the white race. I began thinking I was learning more from him than from any of my teachers at school. The more we talked, the more I looked for examples around me that would back up what he was saying. When a teacher let a Black kid come into class late, something they were pretty strict about normally, I thought, that's what Donny's talking about, the whole favouritism thing.

One night, Donny asked me about my heritage. "Where in Italy was your ancestor from?"

"I don't really know. All I know is we're part English, Scottish, Irish and Italian. Why?"

"I hope she was from the north. Southern Italians aren't pure enough. You should do a DNA test."

I thought Donny was cool, and his group, which I thought of as a secret club, sounded more interesting than hanging around drinking with school kids. Some of his friends—Miles, Luke, Alex, Megan—started adding me on Facebook. One girl, Brianna, was a year younger than me, lived at home and hated the preps at school and the mainstream, just like I did. I don't know how she got into the movement; maybe through her boyfriend, an absent-minded druggie dickhead with whom conversations got really weird. Brianna was kind of obnoxious—but then, so was I. I fit in with her and the others and felt accepted for who I was.

My first actual meeting with Donny took place in early December when he finally came out to Whitby by train. We met at the station, shaking hands as he said, "Nice to finally meet."

"Yeah," I replied, feeling as if I already knew him. "Thanks for coming out." I introduced him to Connor and to Brodie, one of my metalhead friends who was a racist, even though he wasn't involved in the movement. They'd come along because they were curious.

Donny came out to visit me again in January and invited me to be part of his crew, along with Miles, Brianna and about eight other guys. They called themselves SD, from the German word *Sicherheitsdienst*, the intelligence and security division of the German SS and Nazi Party. I liked the sense of importance that came with belonging to a group fighting for a cause, something I'd never felt before.

Donny had told me, "You'll learn more from my friends than from anywhere else," so I was excited to meet them in person. When, later that month, I skipped school to sneak into the city, I marvelled at how they had each other's backs. They accepted each other and me without question, their common goal—the continuation of the white race—bringing them closer to each other than most of the friendships I'd witnessed. Their sense of family was something I didn't feel at home. My mother and brother had always been close and, without my dad's friendship and love, it felt like I didn't have a place in my own family.

I was angry, hurt and rebellious and Donny showed me where to direct my rage. "Immigrants and non-whites are stealing our jobs and teaching our children to be ashamed of their heritage." He took me through several racially and ethnically diverse neighbourhoods in the city, most notably one populated largely by Muslims, where he reinforced the notion of white genocide. "We're being wiped out," he told me as street after street was filled with brown-skinned families. He'd also say things like, "What happened to you in the past (meaning those who hadn't accepted me) is nothing compared to what a non-white will do to you," and, "The non-whites are out to attack our people and culture. Anyone who isn't with us is against us. They're the enemy." I could feel my adrenaline building with each statement. I'd never worried about shades of grey so each comment aligned perfectly with my temperament. I began avoiding interacting with non-whites (easy to do in Whitby) in case they proved me wrong. Since I'd chosen this new identity, I didn't want anyone fucking with it.

Every month or so, Holocaust deniers and history revisionists spoke at meetings held in the conference rooms of Toronto hotels. I skipped school one day and took the train in. "The Jews have fabricated stories of a Holocaust. It's a victim narrative they've created to further their own agenda. There's a Jewish conspiracy," they claimed. "Jews are in control of media outlets. They spread subtle propaganda against us whites."

I believed everything Donny and the others said. I began defining myself as a "white power skinhead," choosing never to use society's terms, neo-Nazi or white supremacist. I refused to use the labels of the mainstream, or "lamestream" as I called it, and distinguished between neo-Nazism or National Socialism, which were about ethnic cleansing; white supremacy, which was about returning to slavery; and white power, which was about segregation, taking back what we'd lost to minorities.

Now that I was part of a crew, I started posting some of my new-found knowledge online, explaining to my friends how they were being duped and telling them the 'truth.' Some would message me: *How can you be into this?* To which I'd reply: *Because I see the truth of how white people are being persecuted in society.* Some chose to remain friends in spite of what I was into but most started to drift away. I still hung out with Brodie, who I think had a crush on me, and Van, who liked

NSBM music too, and I was still dating Connor, but he was becoming jealous of Donny, partly because I wouldn't have sex with him.

Early in February, Regina asked about a post on my page. *Why do you have this on here?*

I answered truthfully. *Because this is what I'm into.*

This led to an online argument between her and Donny through Facebook and Instant Messenger, mostly over my involvement in the movement. When she kept harping: *You shouldn't talk to him,* it got my back up. I had never liked being told what to do and had a hard time believing Regina had my best interests at heart. Besides, I reasoned, Donny had never told me to stop talking to her.

I knew she had a bunch of non-white friends, so one night I challenged her. *What you're lecturing me about—is it for your friends' benefit? Because it's sure not for mine. You don't really care about me.*

She went offline abruptly but she and Donny were soon back to arguing again. Donny had seen a picture of her and her ex-boyfriend, who was Black, so he started ripping on her for that. *You do realize you've contributed to the destruction of the white race by dating someone who isn't white?*

Regina got defensive after that, bitching at me about my beliefs, which I defended aggressively. Donny had taught me how to respond, so when she'd press her point, I'd turn it around and attack her beliefs instead.

When she said: *Your ideology hurts my friends,* I replied: *I don't even know your friends and I don't want to. Your mainstream ideology hurts me but I'm not bitching at you for that.*

It became an endless tug-of-war. Neither of us would let go and eventually I'd had enough, messaging her: *I don't want to talk to you again.* I don't know what was said to the rest of the family but suddenly everyone knew everything, and it seemed like they all took her side because she was the family princess. They proved what I'd known all along—that they'd never liked me anyway. Donny's crew, meanwhile, had proven they were my safe haven by helping me see who Regina really was, assisting me in cutting ties with someone who wanted to control me.

That spring, on a visit to Whitby, Donny gave me a set of Panzer boots. Like Doc Martens, they were steel-toed with white laces but shaped more like clown shoes. These were tangible proof that I was part of the movement, so I made sure to keep them hidden until I turned eighteen in May 2008. Once I was legally an adult, I wore them to school one day. I liked the sense of identity they provided, but more than that I just wanted to wear them. After lunch, the vice-principal pulled me aside. "Let's see the treads on those boots."

I sat down and lifted my foot, displaying the swastika and SS bolts printed on the bottom of the rubber treads. "Do you know what that means?" he asked.

I laughed. "Yeah."

He gave me a big long speech about how unacceptable they were, ending with, "Don't ever wear those to school again."

Things at home had gone from bad to worse. I increasingly believed my mom was screwing me over, trying to keep me quiet and docile by making me feel less than everyone else. Donny had warned me my family would use the argument with Regina against me and it was this prediction, more than his lectures, that convinced me that his way was the right way. On June 22, just days after school finished, my mom gave me an ultimatum: either I start behaving like I wanted to be part of the family, giving up Donny and everything he'd taught me, or she'd throw me out. "You decide," she said. "Who's more important to you, your family or your friends?" It was an easy choice.

JEANETTE

Lauren had been angry and insolent since her father died. But there was a marked change in her behaviour after Christmas. She was suddenly secretive, talking for hours on the extension phone I'd installed in her bedroom. Her two hours of allotted time on the family computer each day grew to four, five or six, something I was unable to police while at work or asleep. Her brother complained that she would scream at him to stay out, even when it was his allotted time. I'd repeatedly warned both kids not to give out personal information on Facebook, to be careful who they contacted, what groups they were involved with, and thought our shared computer would help keep things out in the open. And I, being incredibly naive, had no clue how to search our computer's history to see where she'd been and what she'd been downloading. I thought she was downloading music for her MP3 player. If it was a bit loud and not really my style, so be it.

Lauren began morphing into a vile, antagonistic stranger who'd accuse me of not loving her or taunt me with phrases like, "You don't know the truth" or "History is a lie. The Holocaust never happened." Burying my head in the sand, I avoided confronting the truth, unwilling to find the deeper source of her anger so as not to add to my own grief. I had no idea of the shit-storm brewing.

In January 2008, when Lauren asked if her friend Donny could come out from Toronto and spend a few hours at our place, I was pleased with the opportunity to show my support and invited him to dinner. Of medium build and height, he walked slightly hunched over. He wore a plain T-shirt and jeans so my radar didn't go up until he turned around, his shaved head displaying the tattooed letters 'SD' on his neck. Unaware of their significance, the faded black letters— stark against his pale skin— still sent shivers up my back. *What the hell?* During our drive home from the train station, he answered most of my superficial questions—"Where do you live in the city? How long have you been there? Do you have family in Toronto?"—but it was obvious that he wasn't interested in making conversation with me nor creating a good impression on Lauren's family. His clipped, offhand answers and abrupt tone gave me the impression he was sneering at our middle-class lifestyle. *I'll bet he enjoys it as long as he doesn't have to work or pay for it.*

When we got home, he and Lauren settled in the den. Donny didn't stop talking, the intensity in his words chilling and somehow frightening. Overhearing some snippets of conversation between them—"taking our jobs," "think they're better than us"—I began to realize there was more to his visit than just friendship. After several hours together in the den neither had moved to sit together nor had he said anything remotely sweet or romantic to her, leading me to think he was definitely not interested in her sexually. What would a guy, older and streetwise, want with a naive young girl from the suburbs? I asked myself. I struggled with the desire to interrupt but I'd allowed him to visit and didn't want to embarrass Lauren so I decided to leave them alone and remain quiet. When, after a tense, uncomfortable dinner, we finally dropped him back at the station that night, I ended up paying for his ticket because he said his card wouldn't work.

Donny visited Lauren at home twice more. The second time he brought a young girl named Brianna—dressed in a black combat jacket, her hair long on one side, shorn on the other, she came in with an attitude a mile wide. I left them alone out of respect for Lauren but, standing in the kitchen, I overheard more urgent talk of "them versus us," this time from Brianna. She seemed to be Donny's sidekick, parroting his phrases with ease. It was a relief to see them leave.

The third and final time Donny came to our home coincided with a visit from Lauren's friend Brodie and boyfriend Connor, both of whom had apparently met him previously. Whether planned or not, I was relieved there were two teenage boys with her, friends who might counteract Donny's influence. At one point, I overheard Donny regaling them with stories of his boots, his language salted with derogatory terms as he described how he had used them to "stomp" a Black man. Passing them on my way upstairs, I heard Lauren say to him, "You can use whatever terms you want to around me but be respectful around my mother." Whew, I thought, maybe there's hope after all.

I'd begun noticing Lauren's use of racist slurs and phrases, her views that "whites are the only people who matter," her insistence that she now knew "the truth" and that I knew nothing of the world and its wrongs. Listening to her was difficult. Humiliated, embarrassed and disgusted, I blamed her newfound beliefs on Donny and his friends. "They're horrible—why are you hanging out with them?"

"They're inclusive. They ask me how my day was, what's going on with me. What's horrible about that?"

I forbade Donny and Brianna from coming into our home, hoping their physical absence might change her views, that Lauren would notice the huge gulf between Donny's lifestyle and the one she'd always known. I refused to admit that she was out of control. That this was more than a passing fad or teenage angst. She just needs some new interests, more support, I told myself.

Early in the new year, Lauren found part-time work at a local arts and crafts store. Since she'd always enjoyed painting and doing crafts, I figured it was a good fit—working among shelves of art supplies she'd be exposed to new creative pursuits that would be a better use of her time than sitting at the computer. Unfortunately, I didn't bargain on them training her to work at the front counter.

"I hate the customers," she'd complain. "They're rude. They bitch about stuff that's not my fault. And their kids are little brats."

"You're going to get those anywhere you work," I pointed out.

"I wouldn't if they'd let me work in the back. That's what I asked for. I hate doing cash. I hate this fucking job and I hate the fucking Blacks who think they're better than me."

Unable to listen to her racist crap any longer, I put my foot down. "I don't want to hear any of that garbage again, do you understand? I don't give a damn what your friends are telling you—I won't listen to that in my own home. Got it?"

I continued to work at building relationships with Paul's family, anxious for my kids to stay connected to their father. I knew Lauren wasn't comfortable with Regina, but it wasn't until she refused to attend a family dinner that the details of their online argument came out. I couldn't convince Lauren that Regina had been trying to help, to save her from getting involved with Donny and his racist beliefs. Being on Facebook, Regina knew more about Lauren's leanings than I did; that she willingly argued with Donny on Lauren's behalf told me she genuinely cared about her. But it was too late—by the time I heard about their spat yet another family bridge had been burned. Even though I was well and truly ticked off at Donny for involving himself in family matters I was equally determined not to let it ruin the fledgling family relationships for my son and myself.

It did though. Suddenly there was a decided chill in the air when we walked into a room. Not that I blamed them. What kind of parent was I to have raised such a horrible person? Perhaps the most open-minded of all of Paul's family, Regina's dad was incredibly understanding and kind—surprising to me, considering the aggravation his daughter had had to contend with. He reassured me that Lauren was under Donny's influence, that she wouldn't have participated in the nasty online arguments unless goaded by someone else.

I hoped college would give Lauren a new focus. Earlier in the year, she and I had driven three hours west of Whitby to tour Conestoga College and check out their cabinetmaking and woodworking program. Lauren moaned the whole way there about how far it was, how she'd be away from her friends. But when we arrived, we were both awed by the woodworking shop, the new tools and the great program. She was accepted for the fall semester, but then she didn't want to go. "It's not the school or program I'm interested in."

"Funny, we were both pretty impressed when we were there."

"I'm not ready for college," she raged. "And it's too far from my friends."

"You'll adjust once you get used to it. And you'll make new friends out there."

"I don't want to make new friends."

We argued constantly. My son, who'd once been Lauren's partner in crime and best bud, had taken to hiding in his room the minute he heard a raised voice—a constant, it seemed, since his dad's death. He couldn't ignore either of us but didn't want to be dragged into our screaming matches and barely spoke a word, even to me. We were on edge constantly, waiting for Lauren to explode, cursing and swearing, slamming doors so hard cracks appeared around them. The hole in the wall where Lauren had thrown the phone was a constant reminder that our home had become a battleground.

I relied heavily on my mother, my friend, my son and my therapist to squeak through each day in one piece. My mom remained steadfast, her love for Lauren never wavering despite her worry and disappointment. I, on the other hand, had forgotten to separate the child from her actions and was distraught that my daughter had morphed into someone I couldn't stand to have around.

Around her birthday, in late May, we settled into an uneasy truce. Balloons were tied to chair backs, gifts and cake were bought and my mom came to dinner to celebrate Lauren's arrival into adulthood. We had a nice evening, traded careful stories of her birth and early years and basked in her few smiles but shortly afterward, the hate-filled rhetoric returned. "Hitler didn't exterminate any Jews. That's bullshit," she'd toss at me. "Goddamned Jews made it up, just like they make up everything so they'll sound like the victims."

Amped up and angry, I wasn't surprised by her adamant refusal to attend the senior prom with Connor. "I don't want to wear a stupid dress. Or go to the prom," she'd insist each time he pressed her. His father even called to ask for my help. "We don't have to rent a limo. But Connor's mother and I feel it would be nice for them to go." Nothing I said swayed Lauren and we argued more as the big day approached. Not about the prom, which I'd already agreed "wasn't her," but about how immature she thought Connor was, how she hated school, her refusal to go to college, her insistence that Donny was great, her own anger and its effect on her brother and me.

We couldn't go on as we'd been, tiptoeing around her disruptive behaviour, locked in constant battle. I had to protect my son and myself, and neither of us could live with who she'd become. We had yet another huge argument just days after school finished.

"Your friends are more important to you than us?"

"They care about me. They don't make me feel like I'm nothing," she replied defiantly.

"You aren't nothing. We've never treated you that way. You're just as much a part of this family as your brother or I."

"You don't give a shit about me," she railed. "You're probably not even my real mother."

"What the hell? Where did you get that from?"

"Prove it, then."

Exhausted by her endless challenges, I felt I had no choice but to give her an ultimatum—either she gave up Donny and everything he'd taught her, or she'd have to leave. I didn't believe she would sacrifice eighteen years of family. "Alright. You decide. Who's more important to you—your family or your friends?"

Lauren began grabbing clothes off the floor, stuffing them into a duffle bag that had been her dad's. Standing in her bedroom doorway, total disbelief washed over me. I felt like the worst parent in history as she brushed past me and walked out.

Sobbing, I realized I'd failed my child.

CHAPTER FIVE

1488

LAUREN

I went straight to Connor's house. His dad, Bob, said he'd let me stay there for as long as I wanted, even though his mom worried I'd turn her son into an atheist, which he already was, and one of Connor's sisters knew about my new beliefs and didn't like me hanging around with her brother. Within a couple of days, I was depressed and didn't want much to do with Connor, who finally broke up with me. "Our lives are going in different directions," he said. I pretended I didn't give a shit but deep down I was pissed off. A friend later told me our break-up was mostly about my refusal to have sex.

Four days after I arrived, Bob confronted me, having just spoken to my mom and his daughter. "Are you into that white power shit?"

"Yes."

"You can stay here one more night but then you have to leave," Bob said. "I don't care what you do. You can go hang yourself and I won't care."

Connor didn't speak up for me, which hurt. I thought he was a pansy with no balls, so I decided to leave right then, even though it was nearly midnight. As I walked away, Connor had the nerve to ask, "Are we were still friends?"

I spent the night at Brodie's house. I don't think his parents knew what I was into and luckily they weren't home, so I didn't have to explain myself. Brodie liked me and I'm sure he wanted to take Connor's place as my boyfriend; he'd pretended interest in the whole white power thing but I knew he wasn't serious about it. He was a racist, something he said he'd learned from his dad, and liked the idea of being part of something, but he was too lazy and selfish to make a real commitment. His last words to me when I left the next day were, "Keep in touch."

Donny met me at the Whitby station and we took the train back to Toronto. For the next couple of days, we bunked in the basement of an internet café at the intersection of Yonge and Bloor Streets, sleeping on blankets on the floor along with two or three other people. It was owned by a guy named Bryan whose other business was running credit card fraud out of his storefront. I think he let us stay there out of pity; as far as I knew, none of us were paying him anything. I'd always known Donny didn't have a job and that he was homeless and I believed him when he said it was the fault of immigrants. Rob, an overweight guy in his late twenties who was also staying there, knew where we could wash our clothes for free, Donny used fraudulent credit cards to buy stuff and I got a job at a nearby grocery store to pay for food. It wasn't great but at least we weren't on the street and we were free to hang out with our SD crew. Donny taught me how to arm-bar, hip-throw and hit with force, then made me the group's enforcer.

Dillon, a friend of Donny's, offered us the use of his grandmother's place. Donny had known Dillon's family for years and he frequently crashed there. Even though Dillon's grandmother knew what we were involved in, she never objected and even cooked for us. I gave her some money for my share of the rent and food and I think Donny gave her some of his welfare cheques.

Dillon was associated with the Hammerskins, a more upscale white power group that cultivated a mainstream image. He was their pretty boy, a good-looking, well-dressed guy responsible for attracting recruits, particularly hot women interested in hanging out with the guys. His friendship with Donny went way back so he didn't care that our SD crew wasn't part of the Hammerskins organization, but that didn't stop him from telling me, "You should leave these guys and come with us."

A week or so after I started working at the grocery store, Brodie showed up out of the blue, asking to stay at Dillon's grandmother's with Donny and me. His story was that his parents had tossed him out, but I think he got angry and left on his own. A couple of days later, Donny told me he wanted to meet Brodie alone. Someone had stolen Dillon's grandmother's debit card and cracked the PIN; Brodie was the prime suspect.

"Why would you do that?" he told me he'd asked Brodie.

Brodie had played dumb. "Why would I do what?"

"Steal $700.00 from her bank account. I know you did it. So, where's the money?"

I didn't know what to think. I knew Brodie was conniving and good at instigating things but, when called out, would act like the victim. But was he smart enough to do something like that?

Brodie was scared of Donny and begged me to leave with him, hounding me almost continuously for two days, without mentioning that Dillon's grandmother had already told him he had to go. "Can we move in with your mom? I don't want to stay in Toronto."

"Then go home to your parents' place."

"I can't. But we could both move into your mom's place."

"I want to stay here where I can be more involved in the movement."

Finally, I got tired of the badgering. It was the second week of July; I'd only been in Toronto since June 28, and in that short time so much had happened that I just didn't care anymore. To shut him up, I compromised and we moved to a cheap motel, the Palace Arms, in downtown Toronto.

None of us knew who'd taken the debit card but Brodie seemed the easiest to blame and Donny began sending him harassing emails. I wanted to prove that I was still committed to the movement, even though I was living with Brodie, so I decided to get a tattoo. I'd never been one to think beyond the moment and this day was no different. I had Donny cut my hair on one side of my head into an undercut on the left side and then got "1488" tattooed on that side of my neck. 1488 was a common white power symbol: "14" for the fourteen sacred words, "We must secure the existence of our race and a future for white children," and "88" for Heil Hitler or HH, H being the eighth letter of the alphabet. Brodie got the same tattoo inked on his back, probably to show his "commitment" to me more than anything else.

On the afternoon of July 12, three weeks after I'd left home, a Black cop from the Durham Regional Police Service came to see Brodie and me at the motel. Detective Paisley said my mom had asked them to check on me, and that Brodie's parents had been looking for him too. I told them I'd call my mom, which I did later that day, telling her, "I'm fine. Stop bugging me, okay?"

Two weeks later Detective Paisley and another cop came looking for Brodie. "Your father is concerned. He hasn't heard from you in five days," he explained. His female partner asked if we wanted a ride back to Whitby, but I declined. Donny had taught me not to trust cops, claiming my dad was the exception because of his specialized work. Brodie promised them we'd take the GO train out the next day and I finally gave in. Somehow, between his nagging—"Can we stay with your mom?"—and my mom's emails saying we could work things out, I was sick of hearing how great it would be to give Whitby another try. I didn't have a cellphone so I couldn't tell Donny I was leaving the city until I was back home. His only response was, "What did Brodie say to make you go back there?"

My mom met us at the train station. She wasn't impressed with my undercut hairstyle and tattooed neck. "What is that?" she asked, pointing to the inked numbers. When I told her what they meant, she yelled, "That's a slur against everything you've been raised to believe. My father fought against Hitler so you could have freedom. And that's what you do with it?"

Donny had told me that my grandfather, a bigot and a racist, had probably been conscripted and wouldn't have understood that he was fighting
on the wrong side of those beliefs. I believed him because my history
teacher had once told us conscripts didn't have a choice. "You don't
even like your father," I threw back. "Why are you defending him? It's my
tattoo. Leave it alone. If you don't like it, you don't have to look at it."

My mom wanted me to speak with someone who could get me to
change my mind about the white power movement so she took me
to the police station to speak with Detective Paisley, the cop who'd
shown up in Toronto. He was the wrong person—Black, with an ego
the size of a football field, he was condescending to everyone, even
his coworkers. The way he spoke to other people pissed me off and
he was really critical of everything I said. His attitude was like, Black
cop takes down the Nazis. He didn't ask questions, he just preached
and spent a lot of time ripping on my appearance. My opinions
didn't matter and, if anything, his little speech convinced me to stay
in the movement. I spent the whole time thinking, Do you really
think you'll pull me out of the group by insulting me?

I told Donny about it over the phone that night. "He seriously
thinks he can shame me and that it will change my mind. Fuck him."

Because he had no place to go, Brodie stayed at our place and, for
the five or so weeks he lived with us, he was a pain in the ass. "Be
with me," he'd say, coming into my room in the early morning and
climbing on top of me. When I'd refuse, he'd walk away like a dog
with its tail between its legs or complain to my mother that I hated
him. His harassment went on every day, but I didn't think my mother
would believe me so I stayed quiet. Within a week of coming home I
was fed up with him, especially when he continued ragging on about
Dillon's grandmother's debit card. He messaged Dillon on Facebook
one day: *Yeah, I think Lauren stole it.*

Dillon, of course, messaged me: *It looks like he's trying to blame you,
make all of us turn against you.*

I didn't know what to think. Dillon had always been upfront with me. I wondered if Brodie was trying to get me to leave the SD crew or get kicked out of the movement altogether. Either way, I was done with him. I knew he'd lie if I confronted him, so I completely ignored him instead. Maybe that was worse, because a couple of days later he said, "I'm heading up north to visit friends. See you later."

The next day, September 2, I got a message from his cousin Casey, whom I'd met at school. She'd obviously seen my Facebook profile and the picture I'd posted of my tattoo because she said: *Enjoy that hate symbol on your neck. When people look at it they're going to think, Wow that girl made a lot of mistakes when she was younger. Bingo, they've got it.* I don't think it was a coincidence that she messaged me right after Brodie had left town. I'm sure she hated that her cousin was hanging around with me. Maybe if you'd given him a place to live, I thought, I wouldn't have had to put up with him.

Casey's younger brother had been trying to chat with me online. I didn't want to talk to a twelve-year-old about kid stuff so I kept brushing him off politely but now Casey accused me of trying to recruit him. I responded: *Why would I be interested in recruiting a twelve-year-old? We only take hardcore nationalists, so why you think we'd be interested in your brother is beyond me.*

She didn't believe me and kept after me, warning me to leave her brother alone. I knew she was setting me up, trying to get me into trouble, and it worked. I pushed back: *You probably wouldn't have the balls to try anything if we were out in public.* Then I went on a long-winded attack against her, implying she'd get hurt or maybe wind up dead if she didn't shut up. I ended it by typing the last paragraph in German, using Google translate. She reported me to the cops the next day, and my mom and I were invited to the station for another chat with Detective Paisley on September 6.

I didn't like his attitude any more than I had the first time. His first words to me were, "So we meet again." Again, he picked on my hair and tattoo. "How many girls have a half-shaved head and tattooed neck?" he kept saying. "You're young and pretty, blah blah blah." What he was really saying was, "Why can't you fit in with other girls your age?" He was telling me not to judge people by their appearances, even as he was doing just that. He warned me not to have any contact with Casey and droned on and on while I tuned him out. Eventually he issued me with a formal warning about threatening and criminal harassment, explaining that I could be arrested and charged if I contacted Casey again for any reason. "Who do you think we're going to believe—you or her?" That just confirmed what I already knew, that all of "them"—non-whites and the institutions that supported them—were conspiring against "us," the defenders of white rights.

My mom sat in the interview room with me and cried when Detective Paisley read what I'd written to Casey. Afterward, she started treating me like a ten-year-old, putting a lot of restrictions on me, issuing a curfew, threatening to shut down my email and Facebook profile and telling me not to have anything to do with the movement and Donny. She even tried to force me to get rid of the neck tattoo but there was no way I could afford it. Those rules just pushed me further towards white power.

The next day, we started arguing again. "Follow the rules or you're out."

I grabbed my stuff, opened the front door and stood on the threshold. "I'd rather drink drain cleaner then stay here and put up with this shit."

My mom went to the kitchen, grabbed the bottle from beneath the sink and tossed it at me. "Go ahead. Drink it."

When I tried to throw it back at her, she pushed me out, closing the door while saying, "You can come back when you stop all this nonsense."

I gave her the Nazi stiff-arm salute as I walked away, my hastily packed duffel bag in my other hand.

The next day I messaged Casey, even though I wasn't supposed to: *Thank you for being a bitch. You accuse us of being manipulative yet you went and played all kinds of games in front of the cops. You're the one who instigated the whole debate.* She'd proven to me that people really were out to get us.

JEANETTE

Connor's dad called me to say Lauren was with his family, so I knew she had a decent place to sleep and had eaten well for those first few days. Tearfully, I'd written her an email hours after she left, an apology for forcing the issue. I had no illusions that it would change months of hurt, but it made me feel slightly better to put into words what I hadn't been able to say. *I'm so sorry. I love you but I can't live like this. I want things to be the way they used to be. I want the old Lauren back.* Lauren's reply was terse and nasty, just as she'd been while living at home. She was going to Toronto to get a job and live with Donny. It was then I realized that she needed time on her own and the opportunity to decide for herself what path her life should take.

Still, I worried incessantly. What if she were killed? Beaten or raped? What had I let her get involved in? Always in the back of my mind were thoughts of Paul's disappointment in me, as if somehow he was watching, seeing how badly I'd screwed up parenting his daughter. When Regina's parents came for dinner, I sobbed pitifully about having failed not just Lauren, but Paul and our son as well. Surprisingly, Regina's father gave me the encouragement I needed most of all. "Don't shut her out," he said. "Keep the door open. She'll come back when she's ready."

I heard nothing more from Lauren and my resolve to give her time only lasted a few days. Late on the evening of July 1, I called Durham Police to report her missing. Soon after, they told me they'd located her at Dillon's grandmother's house and gave me the phone number so I could call her myself.

"Don't send the police to check on me," she said when I finally got through.

"Why not?"

"Just don't."

I told her she could come home, that if they were behaving horribly towards her—visions of white slavery, prostitution and abuse ran through my head constantly—she could ask for help and I'd be there. I tried to make her see Donny for the recruiter he was, insisting he didn't care about her, just the movement. But all she said was, "I'm okay. Just stop calling and checking up on me."

Was Lauren being held against her will? Was my interference making Lauren's situation worse? Causing her trouble? She was eighteen and had chosen to live away from home. Unless she asked for help, I had no choice but to honour her wishes.

After more than a week with no contact, I called the police station where Paul had worked and asked for one of his old buddies. "Could you ask around, see if she's okay?"

"Sure," he replied. "I'll talk to the guys downtown, see what we can find out."

Later that week, he called me back. "Lauren's okay. She's staying at the Palace Arms Hotel on King Street West with her friend Brodie." Thank goodness, was my first reaction. At least she was still alive. She called me soon afterward, again asking to be left alone.

When she agreed to come home, I thought it was because she'd realized the movement was wrong, that her family wanted her back and would accept her no matter what she'd done. I was more than willing to try again, to give her the attention she needed, to prove that I still loved her—if only she would meet me halfway.

Those notions quickly died when I saw Lauren at the train station. I was repulsed by her tattoo, even though I didn't understand its significance. Until that moment, I hadn't really let myself believe she was involved with white supremacists. Faced with the truth, my blood boiled. It riled me to think my own flesh and blood was siding with a mass murderer's way of thinking, that my daughter would blatantly throw her British heritage in my face. In spite of my feelings towards my father, he and others in his family had fought against hatred and oppression in World War II. I'd grown up hearing how he'd laid his life on the line for future generations, how he and other veterans deserved respect for their sacrifices, something with which I agreed.

That tattoo also meant that I could no longer hide the fact, from myself or anyone else, that she was a member of the white supremacy movement. Any one of our friends or neighbours could see the blatant symbol of hatred etched into her skin. I cringed to think how they'd judge her or me, a parent who'd raised a racist. How the hell had we ended up here?

I took Brodie in to show Lauren I was willing to accept her friends, but he was a pain in the ass from the start. The futon I'd bought for "his" room—the spare bedroom that usually doubled as an office/craft room—wasn't comfortable enough so I bought another. That wasn't good either so I finally purchased a single bed with a good mattress and made it clear that would be it. He followed Lauren around like a puppy.

I quickly realized Lauren hadn't given up any of her white power views. In fact, she'd go into the city to see her crew several times a week, coming back enraged, spoiling for a fight. I'd hoped Detective Paisley would drag her back to the family who still loved her but their conversation went downhill quickly. Within minutes it seemed he'd pushed her further away from us, right back into the arms of the movement, using lines that might have worked on other wayward kids but that I knew would never work on Lauren. I wanted to smack him for his smug attitude.

Our next meeting with Detective Paisley, on September 6, shook me to the core. According to the police report, Casey had asked Lauren to stop "recruiting" her younger brother via Facebook. Lauren had replied with threats, some written in German. After reading that message aloud, the detective wrote in his notes, "Jeanette Manning was shocked by the tone and language of what her daughter was saying."

He was right—I fell apart. I just could not believe my child had spoken such vile, filthy words, that she could be charged with uttering threats and criminal harassment. I saw in that moment that she hadn't changed. She hadn't even tried.

Lauren, a "self-admitted member of a white supremacist group, National Socialists" was "formally warned" not to have any association or communication with Casey, who'd been advised to contact police after also receiving threatening messages via Facebook from "Blood Flag," an unknown user. The detective's notes stated, "I cautioned Lauren that her ideology is reprehensible, that many in society will have a strong reaction." Further on he noted, "She was cautioned that she could have chosen not to respond but it was apparent that she needed to forcefully articulate her racist views with violence."

I realized Lauren wasn't ready to live with us again. As much as she hated me, her need to hate Blacks, Jews and non-whites was stronger. She hadn't been away long enough to understand how good she had it at home. And perhaps I wasn't ready to forgive and forget what she'd done, what she'd already put us through.

CHAPTER SIX

The Crew

LAUREN

The day I left home for the second time it was pouring rain. As it was Sunday, there were fewer buses so I circled back and stole my brother's bike from the garage, riding it to the train station where I left it unlocked on the racks. I was angry about having wasted so much time and effort on my family. They believed everyone but me, I thought. Why couldn't they see what Regina and Casey and Brodie were like? During the train ride to Toronto, I made a conscious effort to think of Donny. The SD crew had fallen apart while I was in Whitby but I knew I'd be welcome in Donny's new crew.

I took the subway to the internet café, where Donny was once again staying, relieved to see a friendly face. When I told him I'd been kicked out again he said, "I knew it. I was expecting that. You can stay here in the basement with me." We talked briefly about what had happened in Whitby—Butt Fuck Idaho as I called it then—then put it aside to plan my first night back. That evening, we partied with the new crew in Vaughan, north of Toronto. We all pitched in for dinner at the local Boston Pizza and then followed it up with copious amounts of alcohol, an uncomplicated good time for once.

The only remaining members of SD were me, Donny and Miles. The rest were seventeen- or eighteen-year-olds who worked part-time and went to school, or friends of Miles who adopted the rhetoric but were really only interested in metal music. I was the only female in the crew most times. Others came and went, but few stayed. We'd get into street fights with anyone who gave us trouble;

all it took was for someone to yell "Nazi scum" and we'd start brawling. We also spent a lot of time partying in the forests or wooded areas, pretending to be Vikings, setting up bonfires and drinking lots of alcohol, always a big part of our get-togethers. As far as I knew, no one in the crew did street drugs so I never told anyone I'd played around with weed and hash and tried acid once. It was never really my thing anyway.

Miles and Donny were our leaders but most of us listened to Miles, by far the smarter of the two. Miles always wore combat boots but had no patches, so he looked like most other metal dudes, while Donny had tattoos but never wore the boots. I was the only one who looked the part of a skinhead, dressed in T-shirts, cargo pants and Panzer boots, with the under-shaved hair and my one tattoo, 1488. I thought if I wore this angry mask, this badass persona, everyone would be afraid of me and that no one can harm me. I'd have a safe space inside my head where my fears could hide, where nobody could touch them.

Since I'd been the enforcer in our SD crew, Donny appointed me this crew's enforcer too, in charge of beating up anyone who needed it and keeping the drama in check. I'd never even felt in charge of my own life; now I spoke at our crew meetings, using aggressive language to keep the guys' interest. They respected me and listened to me. Quite a few of them said they wished there were more girls out there like me, which made me feel pretty damned good. I felt validated, powerful and smart. I belonged and, after years of being ignored, it was heady stuff.

Enforcement mostly consisted of verbally abusing anyone who stepped out of line. Even Donny. One day, after he'd repeatedly ripped the elastic out of my hair, I told him, "It was funny the first twenty times but fucking stop it." I went outside and had a cigarette to try to calm down. When that didn't work, I went back inside and slapped the side of his head with my open hand.

He yelled. "What the fuck!"

"Stop pulling on my hair."

It didn't stop him, but it made me think. If he was such a pain in the ass to me, it was no wonder no one else really listened to him. If I was pissed at him, there had to be others just as fed up with his stupidity. I began to see that he was causing most of the group's drama. Maybe, I realized, that was why SD had disbanded.

I'd been staying at the internet café for a week when Rob, who was still staying there, tried to assault me. I didn't know him well, but I didn't like his arrogance. He cornered me in the back room, telling me I should grow out my shaved hair, lose the boots and start looking like a girl. Of course I told him, "Fuck no."

He said, "But you'd look so much hotter," then tried to grab my wrist.

I knew his intention was rape. Luckily, I knew how to twist his arm and throw him backwards. As he lay there, two of my friends ran back to see if I was okay, totally ignoring Rob, who lay on the floor writhing with a dislocated shoulder. It was weird accepting their high-fives; I hadn't done anything out of the ordinary, other than look after myself. I felt like I'd been party to something disgusting and vile, an invasion of my private boundaries, and it became even harder for me to trust anyone.

Rob was afraid to speak to me after that, except for one instance weeks later when he told me again to lose the boots. I replied, "You look like a pedophile." He was pissed, and I was relieved when he slunk away. I'd heard other girls hadn't been so lucky, that he was up on sexual assault charges. I'd gotten off easy.

I found a job washing dishes at a fifties-style diner within a week of returning to the city. On September 16, after my shift ended, Donny and I took the train to Whitby to stay the night with Van, my high school friend who'd been into NSBM, racism and politically incorrect jokes, just like me. All the way there, Donny went on about getting back at my mom for the "abuse" I'd suffered at home, taking some of the stuff I'd told him, including the drain cleaner incident, out of context.

"She screwed you over by kicking you out," he argued.

I just wanted him to shut up. "I want as little to do with my family as humanly possible."

I was sure, because of their shared interests, Van and Donny would get along. But they clashed soon after we arrived. Van was smart and knowledgeable about politics, but Donny wouldn't listen to him. I didn't want to get involved in their debate, so I went outside to smoke, where Van eventually joined me.

"Donny's got a few screws loose, hasn't he?"

Donny appeared, mouthing off at us for smoking. "What would Hitler think of you?" He'd said this to me before when my behaviour wasn't what he'd expected.

"Shut the fuck up," I told him.

Now Van turned away, saying, "I'll wait for you inside, Lauren."

"Poxy bitch," Donny sneered at me. I didn't know what that meant and frankly, I didn't care. I also didn't care that he wanted to leave.

"Do whatever the hell you want," I told him. "I'm staying here tonight."

Donny walked away and I rejoined Van, telling him over a few drinks what had happened between my mom and me, about Donny's determination to get back at her. "He's taken everything I've said out of context. I've always resented my mother for not standing up for me with my grandfather, but not enough to seek revenge."

"Well, Donny's left. Where do you think he's gone?"

It was after midnight and the trains to Toronto had stopped running. I did wonder where Donny had gone, what kind of trouble he was getting into, but I was so desensitized to his bullshit antics that I didn't really care too much. He could do stupid things, like breaking a window, on a whim or calculated, planned stuff like thefts, but most of his ideas fell through. I was always surprised when one actually worked. Eventually, Van and I decided to go look for him. We checked the park across from Van's, a five-minute walk from my mom's house. When he was nowhere to be found, we roamed the neighbourhood, even walking past my mom's—I felt numb seeing my old home—in case he'd tried to smash a window or something. There was no sign of him so we went back to crash at Van's.

Around eight o'clock the next morning I took the train back to Toronto and the café. Sure enough, Donny was there. I said, "We went looking for you."

His eyes went wide as he grinned. "I broke into your mom's place," he replied, wound up with excitement. It wasn't just the break-in that had him wired—it was the whole "mission." "Went through the locked side door in the garage, then picked the lock on the inside door."

He'd hinted at theft ever since I'd left home that first time at the end of June. "My mom kept my debit card, credit card and ID 'for safekeeping,'" I'd said offhandedly. "I get why she did that, but eventually I want to get them back."

Now he showed me my mom's Bank of Montreal Mastercard. "Get showered and make yourself look good. We're going shopping."

I hesitated. "How did you get that?"

"Your mom was dumb enough to leave her purse in the laundry room," he said, laughing.

The back of my neck was tingling, a sign something fucked up was happening. I wondered what the outcome of the theft would be and how I was going to trust Donny again. I thought about walking away but realized I wasn't in any position to argue. Donny knew it too. "You're homeless, you've got nowhere else to go. Get dressed."

I showered, dressed and headed out with him to a place on Yonge Street that sold ID cards with swipe stripes and photos, which we would need in order to use the credit card for larger amounts. We took the new ID—bearing my mom's name and my picture—to a Future Shop up near Yonge Street and Sheppard Avenue, in North

York. Donny bought a MacBook, an HP All-in-One Printer, which he planned to sell for cash, and a product service plan. The charge for all three was $2,858.86.

We had no problem at Future Shop but the stores we visited afterward wouldn't take the ID because it looked like it had been issued in another province. "Fuck it," said Donny. We returned to the café, where Bryan offered to buy the stuff from us for $1500.00. After paying Bryan what he owed for his internet usage, Donny used the credit card to buy a train ticket to Whitby for $7.00. "To make it look like Brodie stole your mom's credit card." I didn't point out how stupid that was; neither of us had any idea where Brodie was.

I felt dissociated, removed from it all. Over the years I'd learned to block my feelings, to ignore stuff I didn't want to deal with and any emotion that might make me vulnerable. That had been my coping mechanism for as long as I could remember. Still, I felt unsure, uneasy and in need of reassurance. "Should we have done that? Ripped off my mom?"

"Your mom deserved it."

I was still angry with my mother, but mostly I was focused on living my life. It was Donny who couldn't let it go. Another night he told me about a prank phone call he'd pulled on her.

"What did you say?" I asked.

"I called asking for you. Your mom said, 'I thought she was with you.' I told her I hadn't seen you in a month."

He told me my mom had cried, but I shrugged it off. "She probably doesn't care." Why would she cry? She didn't care about me.

While Donny was laughing, I wondered why he'd bothered to pull such a stunt. She hadn't believed anything he'd said before and a small part of me hoped she hadn't bought into his crap.

That October, someone sent my mother an email full of shit-talk, using a Gmail account with the handle Blood Flag, the same account someone had used to email Casey the month before. I'm not sure if it was Donny or someone else and didn't really care, but I wondered if it was because of another remark I'd made: "If I wanted to teach her a lesson, I'd send her nasty emails."

Donny introduced me to Paul Fromm, a former teacher with ties with the Ku Klux Klan, who we all looked up to. Fromm had founded the Canadian Association for Freedom of Expression (CAFE), which helps racists, anti-Semites and Holocaust deniers being prosecuted for hate crimes. He was also the director of Citizens for Foreign Aid Reform, which opposes foreign aid to developing countries, and the Canada First Immigration Reform Committee, as well as the host of a radio show on the Stormfront website. The *National Post* labelled him "one of Canada's most notorious white supremacists." We called him—and others like him, people in high paying jobs or respectable professions who espoused white supremacy—"suit Nazis."

Fromm reminded me of the character Cameron in the movie *American History X*, a figurehead who spoke while the rest of us did his dirty work. But his handshake was firm and he took a special interest in me. "It's refreshing to meet a young lady who isn't brainwashed by MTV culture." Paul and his then wife, Diane King, were impressed by my dedication to the movement, my ability to throw around the rhetoric. When they asked me to get more involved in events, passing out flyers after his speeches, I felt as if I were someone special, a bit more important than everyone else.

We'd also hand out carefully worded flyers to the general public, flyers advocating for freedom of speech and opposing political correctness without mentioning white power, hoping to connect with people looking for an identity. And Donny, Miles and I would go into Facebook groups looking for the one lost kid who needed a place to fit in. Strangely, even though this was how Donny had introduced me to the movement, I didn't consider myself a recruit.

I'd done most of the research myself on Facebook and Stormfront, so I felt as though I'd earned my place.

I had freedom and no rules, which was what I'd wanted, but the living conditions sucked. Even though I was proud to wear the boots and white laces, the shaved hairstyle and hate-themed tattoo, it was difficult living in the basement of a dingy internet café or surfing on someone's couch. Dinner was the only meal I ate each day, partly in the hopes that I'd lose the extra weight I kept seeing in the mirror but also because I didn't have a lot of money. I felt I belonged in the city, with the movement, but there was still something missing. Most of the other guys, except for Donny, had families they lived with, or at least spoke to. I had no one. Usually, I didn't let that bother me, but once in a while I'd get pissed that their families would let them make their own decisions and run their own lives while my own mother seemed to hate me.

As the weeks wore on, Donny and I started bickering. He could be quite funny and had initially seemed like an older brother or father figure but when he started picking fights with "listo-bums"—people who drank Listerine to get drunk—I began to see he wasn't the person I'd thought he was. When a homeless Native guy overdosed in front of me one afternoon, his face going colourless as I watched, I called EMS and stayed with him until they arrived. I figured that was how you treated another human being. When push comes to shove, you do what needs to be done. This guy was dying right in front of me, his face turning blue as he gasped for air—he needed my help, no matter what his ethnicity.

Donny showed no empathy, and I began to wonder, like Van, if he had his head screwed on right. I didn't find him or his antics funny anymore, so I wasn't upset when, one evening in late October 2008, he took off for British Columbia, saying he was sick of Ontario. He sent endless emails asking me to join him, then called one day threatening to kill himself if I didn't come. I told him I didn't want to, that

I had a good job at the diner that I didn't want to give up. When he called the next day to tell me he didn't do it, that was the breaking point. I finally told him I'd had enough.

JEANETTE

While Lauren was away from home, I received an email from a dear friend, a member of the nearby chapel we'd sometimes attend: *I've asked our prayer group to keep Lauren and your family in their prayers.*

The hairs on my neck prickled. I panicked. Was it possible he knew of Lauren's involvement in white power? Maybe he was referring to her leaving home. Maybe he didn't know anything more. How could he, unless he and Lauren were Facebook friends? These thoughts were immediately followed by a fresh worry. If he did know about her beliefs, how could I keep him from telling anyone else? I emailed back: *No. Please, don't say anything to anyone. I don't want anyone knowing about this.*

It wasn't that I didn't appreciate his prayers, his love or his help. He, along with many of the chapel's congregation, had rescued me at my lowest ebb after Paul's death, giving me hope, faith and love. If anyone could be accepting, forgiving of Lauren's lifestyle, I knew it would be him. My problem was the utter self-disgust and humiliation I felt for having raised a white supremacist. I'd told only my mom and best friend, the two people I trusted most, about Lauren's involvement, the difficulty I had accepting her newfound beliefs and the culture into which she'd submerged herself. How could she prefer life on the streets and the company of racist thugs? How far would she go to prove herself worthy of the cause? More than anything, I was ashamed of *being* ashamed. This was my child I was ashamed of. What a horrible mother I'd become.

I missed the daughter I'd thought I'd known and worried

incessantly, comforting myself by remembering Lauren's immense strength of will and inner toughness. She had Donny and several friends she believed were her family now, father/big brother figures who'd look after her when she couldn't do it herself. More than anything, I knew she'd fight to prove to me how little she needed me in her life. Still, at night I lay awake crying, wondering when I'd get the call to say she'd been arrested, charged with murder or assault. Worse was the image of the police at my door telling me she'd been hurt or killed, either by rival groups, gangs or stray bullets. I dreaded never seeing her again, never being able to hold her and tell her how much I loved her.

Through all of it, I continued working, filling my head with numbers and data, blocking out all else for eight hours each day and half-days on weekends. At lunch hour, I'd walk with a coworker who was a good friend without divulging what I was going through. I tried to act as if nothing was wrong, tried to continue with my life as if my heart hadn't been ripped from my chest. I searched for assistance or information without success. There wasn't much online; even if I'd known what to look for, the white power movement in Canada was still flying under the authorities' radar. I contacted a Jewish advocacy group for help but never heard back. After that, I gave up, figuring ignorance was preferable to knowing exactly what Lauren was involved in.

During the summer, I'd attended my son's twice-weekly baseball games, both of us pretending for a few hours that we were "normal." When school resumed in September, he poured himself into his schoolwork, guitar and driving lessons, having turned sixteen early in the new year. He had a small group of good friends and matured quickly, struggling with the usual teenage issues but he was always there for me. Right or wrong, he'd become the man of the house.

In vain, I tried online dating, hoping it would take my mind off my daily life but soon realized I wasn't ready for it. Later that year, I won a car—a bright red Pontiac Solstice—through the local hospital's lottery. It was a great little vehicle but after three months, I sold it and banked the money. After losing both Paul and Lauren, I didn't feel I deserved it.

The night Donny broke into our home, I woke up suddenly, afraid someone was in the house. Hearing nothing but a faint click, I fell back into an uneasy sleep. The next morning, when my son needed money for a school trip, I retrieved my purse from its usual spot in the laundry room and realized someone had stolen my credit card, health card and a Canadian Tire gift card worth $1200.00. There were no signs of forced entry nor was anything else taken. Cold fear lodged inside me . . . right before white-hot anger took its place. I knew immediately that Donny, and possibly Lauren, had been involved. I wondered how much of it had been her idea.

I called the police, anger fuelling my decision to blow the whistle on them. There was no way I was going to sit back and play the victim. It was bad enough they'd stolen my identity, but breaking into my home, my sanctuary, was just too much. The officer I spoke with initially didn't believe me when I said I knew who'd been responsible, which increased my frustration, so I requested Detective Paisley who, thankfully, believed me. After promising to forward whatever information I could obtain, I called the Bank of Montreal, who held the Mastercard; they supplied the details of where and when my charge card had been used. Once I'd given the detective everything, he contacted each of the stores, one of which immediately offered him access to their cameras. Within two days, he had the proof he needed. I'm sure he expected me to relent but my determination never wavered.

"That's my daughter," I told the detective through clenched teeth, as we sat in a tiny, airless interview room viewing the grainy surveillance footage of my daughter fraudulently purchasing thousands of dollars worth of electronics in my name. Watching Lauren hand over my credit card, her accomplice lurking at the bottom of the screen, I added angrily, "And that's Donny."

"Do you want to press charges, Mrs. Manning?"

I had hit rock bottom. "Yes."

Lauren would have to deal with two charges of Possession/Use of a Credit Card, one count of Fraud Under $5,000, one count of Impersonation with Intent, one charge of Forgery and one count of Possession of Property Under $5,000. Due to staffing constraints and distance, he warned me it would take some time to process everything, locate and serve Lauren and Donny and try them at the Oshawa courthouse. That's fine, I thought. I'll wait.

"Did she do it to teach me a lesson?" I asked my mother that afternoon. "How on earth could she do such a thing to me?" My mom knew everything: every argument, every incident, every painful moment between Lauren, my son and me. She, along with my friend who lived out west, had supported me from the beginning.

"She's hurting," my mother said, sadness evident in her voice. Lauren's drama wounded her as much as me. "And Donny's probably pushing her buttons, egging her on."

On October 23, 2008, I received an email from "bloodflag.1880," an unknown address that immediately had the hair on my neck standing. In part, the opening paragraph, in bold capital letters, read:

SO YE ENJOY TALKING SHIT EH? WELL HAVE FUN WITH THAT AND ENJOY YER SAD LIFE BASED AROUND NOTHING BUT STATUS AND POOR ATTEMPTS IN BRINGING OTHERS DOWN. YOU ME DEAR MADE A HORRIBLE ATTEMPT AT TRYING TO RUIN SOMEONES LIFE AS IT DID NOT WORK IN THE LEAST AND I MUST SAY THAT YOU KNOW NOTHING AS TO WHAT WE DO WHATSOEVER.

Two pages of skinhead culture and history followed, clearly cut and pasted from elsewhere, before the writer continued:

As for your little "nazi-lover" names for your daughter which i was laughing at the second i heard it...well is that not what the 88 means on her neck. HEIL HITLER. It can also refer to the 88 precepts in the book mein hampf (sic) which by the way there are many bias copies of it now a days thanks to the liberal mind set that you seem to have....You may also choose to believe that Lauren is insignificant to us and we are only using her to promote our scene by having an attractive girl in it but you my dear are horribly mistaken. Even if we did brainwash people (which we don't) we would never even had to think about doing that to lauren... we are all friends in this.....we are the ones who give each other strength and encouragement to move forward with our lives and our ideas...so in short my dear, have fun talking shit about lauren.

Had Donny written it? Or had Lauren been the author?

CHAPTER SEVEN

A New Crew

LAUREN

When I first met Raymond in November 2008, I was working afternoon shifts at the diner. He appeared rough, his face hard, his eyes
cold and dead looking. His bomber jacket and faded jeans didn't stand
out but his black boots and white laces caught my eye. He'd come into
the café with a friend and referred to the Korean waiter as "a lousy
immigrant." He's one of us, I thought. I noticed him staring at my
boots and laces, so I went over to introduce myself.

"Hi," I said, "Have I met you before?" I noticed the tattoo on his right
hand, tucked in the webbing between his thumb and first finger—a
solid black swastika. I'd seen that before, but never on someone's hand.

"No, but I think I have you on Facebook," Raymond replied. We
often added people we didn't know but who shared our beliefs.

For the next two or three weeks, he hung out at the café a lot and
soon we began dating. I was desperate to prove to myself that I was
straight so dating a dude I liked felt right. I had become good at
denying my interest in women and hadn't met any females I found
attractive anyway. Fresh out of prison—he told me he'd been inside,
but I didn't ask what he'd done because it wasn't anything new for
"our people" to be jailed—Raymond was living in a shelter on welfare. Since I was working but still crashing at the café, we decided
to get a place together, more to have a place to live and party than
to be living together. Between us we were barely able to afford a tiny
bachelor apartment in Toronto's Vaughan and Oakwood district—
ironically, a predominantly Black area of the city.

We were often in conflict with others in the neighbourhood. One day on the bus, a Black guy at the back yelled "Fucking Nazis" after we sat down in the front seat. He made more derogatory comments until Raymond got up, walked towards him and gave him the Heil Hitler salute, motioning, Come on, hit me first. He'd always start fights like that so, if challenged, he could say he hadn't thrown the first punch. The guy pulled a knife and they began to fight. I could hear some of the other riders complaining and little kids asking their moms what was happening. After less than a minute, the driver stopped the bus and threatened to toss us all off.

Shortly after we settled in, a childhood friend of my mom's included me in a group email, a joke she'd sent to several people. I replied: *Ha ha, thanks*, and she wrote back: *Contact your mom*. That made me stop and wonder who'd died; I figured that would be the only reason my mom would want to talk to me. We hadn't spoken for months and, after she'd thrown me out that last time, I'd decided I'd never speak to her again. I wasn't sure if or how she'd respond to me now but I sent an email anyway and was surprised when she wrote back. It was nice that she wasn't mad or yelling at me so I replied that I was alright, that I had a job and a place to live and was no longer in contact with Donny. I even admitted she was right about him, saying: *One thing I have to hand you is that you were right about him, he is a joke*. But further down, I also wrote: *As you can figure, NS (National Socialist) will always be in my views.*

My mom replied: *You mentioned being surprised that I would write you back . . . it's been very difficult for us these last few months—actually, the past year—but I still love you and know that the daughter I'm proud of is still there somewhere. We were very disappointed and upset with the breaking in and stealing of my cards, etc . . . but my love doesn't go away—I'm not my father.*

I thought it was worth a shot to keep emailing her, to keep our only means of communication open, until she asked me to apologize to

Regina and her family. I put the brakes on then: *Fuck no. I'm not bending over and taking it.* I'd emailed my mom to talk to her, not to the rest of the family, none of whom had bothered with me since I left home.

Soon after we moved in together, Raymond's true personality started to come out. He'd often call me "a dumb cunt," saying I wasn't cut out to be part of the movement. "Just go back to mommy," he'd sneer. One night he scrolled through the messages on my phone, then accused me of looking at another guy. "You're looking at him. You're cheating on me," he yelled, even though he'd found nothing.

"How can I do that when the only time I leave is to go to work?" I shot back.

He threw my CDs and things across the room, intending to break them. While he threatened to hurt me physically, he never went through with it. But the verbal abuse felt just as bad.

Raymond and I caused some trouble around our new neighbourhood, vandalizing stuff and yelling anti-Semitic comments at passers-by. We formed a new crew with Miles, from Donny's last crew, Bentley, who I knew through Donny, and Raymond's friend Isabelle.

Bentley, whose first name was Andrew, was a decent guy, around twenty-five, who loved the sound of his own voice. He had been thrown out of the Hammerskins for supposedly taking fifty or sixty pictures at any given event, which had led them to think he was an informant. He had his own place down near the lakeshore and worked at the Pickle Barrel restaurant, which meant he was better funded than most of us. Of average build, he dressed like a punk/skinhead, his leather jacket peppered with patches, his short dark hair usually styled in a Mohawk.

Isabelle's daily uniform consisted of jeans, tank-tops and combat boots. She had short hair, dyed blond, and lived with her dad in the Woodbine Beach area. Sixteen years old, she'd been kicked out of school for throwing something at another student so she spent her days hanging with us.

Raymond insisted we call ourselves the Toronto Storm Troopers. We all thought it sounded fucking stupid, like something from *Star Wars*, so we remained nameless but tried to model ourselves after Calgary's Aryan Guard. Hooligans like us, they were into causing trouble and hurting people. We thought they were badass for the way they stood up for the movement, often approaching and debating those who challenged their ideals. I met a few of them in person but most of our contact was online—Facebook and Messenger—because we didn't have the money to travel.

Our apartment became the crew's meeting place. Bentley and I were the "intellectuals," sitting around citing examples of the brainwashing of the middle class while the others listened and spewed, "I hate everyone who isn't white." Raymond, whose father was supposedly a Ku Klux Klan member, tried endlessly to prove whites had built our civilization, often saying our ancestors would be ashamed of society as it was now. But mostly he was obsessed with boots. "If you don't have boots and laces," he'd say, "then you're not committed." I wore mine because I liked them, but also because I had nothing else.

My mom and I had been emailing back and forth and I was feeling a bit more comfortable with her, but not enough to tell her everything I was doing. She asked me not to come home for Christmas, saying it was too soon for us to try to rebuild our relationship. I agreed but got in touch after the holidays, thinking she could come see our place: *If you want to come, you can.* I wanted to prove that I could make it on my own. When the day came, she called to say the basement had flooded and she couldn't travel into Toronto, so Raymond and I took the train out to Whitby and met her at a family restaurant for dinner. On our way back to the city hours later, I realized I wasn't angry with my mom anymore. That had somehow dissipated when we'd started emailing. I also realized how much I missed home, but I didn't say anything about that to Raymond.

At first, I thought I had finally found a home and a great crew, but

I soon found I wasn't cool with the coke and ecstasy they were doing in addition to weed and alcohol. Miles was heavily into booze, like me, and Raymond and Bentley had probably always done drugs, but this was the first time I remember them getting so fucked up. Life was a constant party and it was starting to get old. It was the same shit every day.

I began seeing myself jumping in front of the subway train or putting a gun to my temple. I didn't know what was causing these thoughts and never acted on them, but they scared me enough to send me looking for help. Sitting in a small, windowless room, I told the doctor at CAMH, Toronto's Centre for Addiction and Mental Health, that I was confused and couldn't sleep, listing my symptoms but not divulging how I'd got them. He tried to diagnose me but I didn't fit into any of his categories so he suggested talk therapy: meeting with a therapist to see my problems from a different perspective, then learning to alter how I looked at them. I wanted a quick fix, an overnight solution, not long-term therapy. In the end he gave me a prescription for sedatives, warning me not to mix them with alcohol. But I drank anyway and the combination made my head spin. I made the mistake of confiding in one of my movement friends and he lectured me about pills being "the government's form of control to keep us docile." When they ran out, I didn't bother to refill the prescription but continued medicating myself with booze.

Raymond and I began fighting so much I was fired from the diner for missing shifts. Luckily, I still had some money and was able to get welfare to cover my bills and Raymond's cellphone, which I'd put in my name because of his bad credit. With time on our hands, Paul Fromm asked our crew to put printed flyers beneath doors in west-end Toronto apartment buildings where the population was mostly white, hoping to recruit others for the big man himself. These, like the pamphlets Donny and I had distributed, were well worded, professionally printed and devoid of anything that screamed white power. Targeting white people over the age of fifteen or sixteen, or even adults, since Fromm himself was older, we had a lot of doorways to cover. We'd wait until someone opened the front door then hurry in, pushing flyers beneath apartment doors before running away. We always remembered Fromm's advice not to get caught spreading hate—if anyone wanted to know more, they could contact the number on the flyer.

Other than distributing flyers, our version of activism ended with getting into fistfights and intimidating people on the streets. One night in late January we decided to burn a flag of the Soviet Union that hung on the side of a Russian souvenir shop near our apartment. I was used to causing trouble so the whole thing didn't mean much to me.

"I don't like that symbol," Raymond said as fire consumed the hammer and sickle. "It's the enemy." We saw communists, socialists or anarchists as self-hating, anti-racist white people. Miles and I watched as Bentley took pictures of Raymond saluting in front of the burning flag and walked away laughing. Somehow the pictures showed up on Anti-Racist Canada, an anti-hate website, connecting Raymond and the rest of us to the fire; we all ended up on their watchlist.

I'd begun to notice how many disagreements between members of the same crew led to fistfights. One Friday night, a friend of Raymond's named Kennedy, Isabelle and her ex, Rick, a drug dealer who'd just gotten out of rehab, Raymond, Bentley and I were at our place, drinking, hanging out and doing drugs. Bentley and I were having one of our "intellectual" chats while Rick was trying to get Isabelle to date him again. Eventually, Isabelle passed out on our bed and, with us watching, Rick went over and lay on top of her, touching her under her bra and down her pants. Raymond and I pulled him off and started beating him up. In spite of the drugs he put up a good fight. When Kennedy tried to get between us and Rick, he took a blow to the face and hit the floor, unconscious from the hit and the booze.

Rick and Raymond continued fighting and the violence intensified with both of them throwing each other's heads into walls. Kennedy woke up and got between them again; seconds later he was back on the floor, barely able to talk, whispering, "Someone help me." Raymond, like me, was worried Rick wouldn't leave but we were more scared that Kennedy might die. When we stumbled outside, covered in bruises and blood, two Black guys ran towards us, asking if we were okay. Even though we were decked out in hate symbols, they said they wanted to help, calling emergency services and staying with us until the ambulance arrived. They even gave us money for a cab ride back from the hospital.

I was stunned. Why were these guys helping us? Every narrative I'd been taught claimed Black men were out to get us, to harm us, but what had happened was the opposite. Their willingness to assist challenged everything I knew. I'd experienced kindness where there shouldn't have been any. For the first time, I felt conflicted about my beliefs.

In mid-February, Raymond and Isabelle again targeted the Russian souvenir shop, spray-painting hate symbols on the front window in red paint: swastikas, 88 for Heil Hitler and WP for white power. Bentley and I were at the apartment when Raymond returned, bragging about what he'd done, how much he'd enjoyed defacing the store.

Two nights later, we argued again and Raymond went for a walk to cool off. Later he texted me: *I'm about to do something stupid.* When he came back, he said, "I threw a rock through the window of that commie store and ran off." Laughing, proud of himself, he bragged, "And I didn't get caught." That was the third act of vandalism he'd committed against the Russian shop in two weeks. His antics were getting old. What was this doing to further the movement? I asked myself.

Several nights later, I stayed home while Raymond, Isabelle and her friend Allie went to Bentley's place to party, apparently mixing needles with alcohol and ecstasy. The next morning, after Bentley left for work, they all came back to the apartment and Raymond, looking guilty, broke up with me. All he said was, "We're done."

They stuck around for another hour, acting like morons, smoking joints and basically ignoring me. I was pissed that Raymond hadn't said anything more to me and had a feeling he and Isabelle had been together. Why was he leaving me? What did I do wrong that he'd go after someone else? But I couldn't question him in front of the girls and they all took off together.

The following day, Raymond texted me: *Get out. I'm keeping the apartment.* I didn't have a choice because, even though I'd paid more than my share of rent, his was the name on the lease. So, I packed up my stuff and left a note: *Don't bother trying to contact me. You won't be able to.* Then I called Eva's Place, a shelter in North York that I'd found online that afternoon.

Eva's Place was co-ed, dirty and looked a bit like I imagined a prison would look. A shelter where the age range was sixteen to twenty-one, it provided all meals, rooms with two or three bunk beds, clean linens, showers and toiletries. I didn't mind that they kicked us out at nine every morning, letting us back in at four in the afternoon. Nor did I mind the conditions. It was a safe place to sleep.

An hour after I checked into the shelter, two police officers, one male and one female, showed up. Apparently, Raymond had seen my message and, thinking it was a suicide note, had called 911.

"We're checking to see if you're okay," one of them explained.

"Do you plan to tell them where I am?" I asked.

"No. We just wanted to make sure you're still alive."

A week or so passed before I saw Raymond again. I didn't miss any of his or the crew's bullshit. In fact, I was relieved to be away from it all. I'd grown tired of them and was beginning to consider finding a new crew where the members took the movement more seriously. I spent the week hanging out at the café and drinking until

I blacked out, but that night I was half-sober, waiting for Bentley, who'd asked me to meet him downtown. Strangely, he wasn't where he said he'd be. Instead, Raymond, Brianna, Isabelle and another guy I didn't recognize showed up. I hadn't seen Brianna since my days in SD but wasn't surprised to see her—everyone in the movement knew everyone else.

Brianna approached me first. "We're going to make this simple. Take off your boots, give them to us and you're free to go."

Taking off my Garrison boots, which I'd bought myself not long before, would be like symbolically handing in my resignation. Instead, I said, "I'm supposed to meet Bentley. Where is he?"

"Doesn't matter," said Brianna.

"I don't want anything to do with you idiots," I told her.

"That's why you're going to take off the boots and give them to us. Then you can go."

Raymond didn't say a word the whole time, just stood there texting, even when Isabelle piped up, "Oh, by the way, Lauren, Raymond's mine now."

That really pissed me off. I'd suspected something between them, and Bentley had told me a few days before that Isabelle and Allie had had a threesome with Raymond, but being confronted with it directly made me more angry than ever. Now I retorted, "Enjoy my leftovers. I don't care."

I stormed off but I could hear footsteps behind me. Suddenly, I felt someone's hands on my head and neck and, the next thing I knew, I was thrown into a brick wall, my head slamming full force into its rough surface. I fell to the ground and must have passed out because when I came to, dazed and in agony, somebody was restraining me while several pairs of boots were kicking me, my body absorbing blow after blow. I struggled to get up. It was hard fighting all of them, so I went down three more times before I realized one of the guys—trying to shield us from passers-by—held a knife. I lurched to my feet and managed to knock it out of his hands just as a security guard came forward, splitting us up and yelling, "Run!"

Every part of me was hurting—my head pounded, I felt off-balance and shaky, my lip was bleeding, my knees and back throbbed from the kicks and my boots were gone—so it was hard to run. Luckily, the nearest hospital wasn't far away. I must have blacked out a few times while stumbling there because I don't remember much of the journey, nor do I remember passing anyone on the darkened street. When I got to the emergency department, the first thing they asked me to fill out was a police report. I'm sure they'd seen beating victims before, considering the hospital was located in a sketchy part of the city, but still, my first thought was, Oh shit. But for once I did as I was asked.

The emergency room doctor was of mixed race so I was leery of him examining me. Surprisingly, he was kind, treating me like a human being despite my white power tattoo. Gently, he asked, "What happened?"

I whispered, "I got jumped."

All he asked after that was where I'd been hit and with what. Once again, I was thrown off balance. Here was someone I'd been taught to hate who was willing to overlook the differences between us *and* my questionable appearance. I knew I didn't deserve his kindness but was grateful that he'd helped me.

When the cops showed up, they took my statement and then called Bentley.

"Hello? Is this Andrew Bentley? This is Officer Jones. Don't hang up on me because I won't like that too much. I want to know why you asked to meet Lauren but didn't show up."

A few minutes later, after repeatedly asking Bentley for information, he told me, "This Bentley is a piece of shit."

"Why?" I was curious about the cop's opinion. I thought Bentley was a piece of shit too and wanted to compare notes, and since I was pissed at my ex-friends, I wasn't bothered about talking to the police. It was really only Detective Paisley who'd annoyed me anyway.

"He just hung up on me."

When he tried calling back, Bentley's phone was turned off. The officer left the message, "We might come visit you, Andrew. At home or at work." Soon after they told me they'd arrested him at his workplace, in front of his coworkers, on suspicion of him setting up the whole ambush. No one could tell me if Raymond or any of the others would face charges as well, but by then I really didn't care anymore.

I thought the crew beat me because they blamed me for posting the pictures of Raymond's flag-burning online, when in fact it had been Bentley who'd ratted out Raymond. But I hadn't bothered to hide how fed up I was with their drama, so I'd been an easy mark. Suffering from a bad concussion that took months to heal, I was relieved to be out of their crew but determined to find a new one.

Toronto is a big city. You'd think it would be easy to get lost in a sea of people but a few days later I saw Brianna and her boyfriend at Eva's Place, the shelter I now called home. I froze when I met Brianna's eyes, watched her smile at her boyfriend as if to say, Hey we can fuck with her more now. I'd already told the staff about my beating, so I immediately went to the desk and asked them to transfer me someplace else.

"Why?"

"That's one of the people who jumped me that night," I said, pointing at Brianna. The staff member called the police and when they arrived, I watched them take Brianna out to the police car. I'm sure they were checking if she had any warrants out for arrest, then questioning her about my beating. They held her for a short time before one of the officers drove me to the nearest subway station so I could get to Covenant House, another nearby shelter, right away.

The next day, someone from the Aryan Guard messaged me: *You might want to look at Brianna's FB profile. She's slandering you up and down.* I went back to the internet café and there it was, all this stuff she'd written about me being a cop-caller and having a Black boyfriend at the shelter, which was a lie. Other people had commented: *Lauren wouldn't do that stuff.* But she insisted that my new boyfriend was a commie.

Pissed, I messaged her: *First you're saying I'm dating a Black guy. Then you say I'm dating a commie. Why don't you get your story straight, bitch?* She didn't reply.

Covenant House was insanely well-kept. There were two of us in each room and all meals were provided. Although we weren't forced out during the day, we were expected to attend employment searches, school or whatever was listed on the individual plan they'd set up for us. I was supposed to be finding work.

Not long after my arrival, I was hanging out at the Eaton Centre with Nick, a friend I'd met at Covenant House who shared many of my beliefs but didn't dress the part. Nor was he in the movement, despite being pissed off at the world. When I saw Brianna and her boyfriend handing out flyers in front of a store, I froze. As we turned to run, they chased us but Nick, knowing the story of my beating, steered me to the nearest security guard and told him we were being followed. Once they saw him with us, they gave up and walked away.

A few weeks later, I was walking up Yonge Street, happy to be away from the shelter residents accusing each other of stealing their things or looking at them the wrong way. I'd found a lot of people in youth shelters seemed to think they were tough, but most weren't. When I turned the corner, the first people I saw were Isabelle and Bentley. If Isabelle had been alone, I think I would have beaten her up but there was no way I was going to go up against the two of them. Flashbacks of my attack made me turn and run—I'd never had a flashback before and having those events run through my head, like a movie playing over and over again, terrified me. Isabelle and Bentley followed me to

Covenant House where, luckily, some of my new friends were standing around outside. "I'm being chased," I said between gasps.

One of them told me to go inside and, from the safety of the shelter, I watched my friends create a human wall in front of the door. I was freaked out, my heart thumping with adrenaline and fear, my hair standing on end as Isabelle and Bentley eventually turned away. I was pissed at Bentley for being such a follower and angry at Isabelle for turning on me but so relieved to have new friends willing to help.

JEANETTE

I was shocked when an email from Lauren appeared, out of the blue, in my inbox. I opened it with trepidation, wondering if it contained threats, verbal abuse or sneering taunts about the ease with which they'd broken into our house and stolen my cards. After months of silence, I had no idea what to expect and was pleasantly surprised to find the tone of her email markedly different from the anger I'd learned to associate with my daughter. Almost conciliatory, she enquired about her brother and me. After my short, carefully worded reply, her second email sounded almost happy. As if she were indeed content with her new life, her boyfriend, her ability to work and provide for herself. Grateful that she was still alive and rid of Donny, I was nevertheless disappointed when she told me National Socialism would always be a part of her life. Did this mean we could never heal our fractured relationship completely? There was no way I felt ready to accept that part of her into our lives again.

I figured I had nothing to lose in telling her my love hadn't waned, that I knew the daughter I loved was somewhere inside her. Most of all, I needed her to understand and believe that I was not, and never could be, my father. Having been dismissed by him for most of my life, I couldn't possibly imagine doing that to my own child. I'd never considered throwing her out to be equivalent to shunning her, but maybe I was just fooling myself. Either way, I had a tiny window of opportunity and I took it.

Now that we were back in touch, I hoped that Lauren would give my son and me the opportunity to have a better relationship with Paul's family. If not for Lauren's involvement in the movement, her friendship with Donny, I reasoned to myself, she and Regina could have easily ironed out any issues they had. If she would just apologize, perhaps we could have that closeness, that sense of family I was looking for.

It wasn't Lauren's adamant refusal that led me to exclude her from Christmas, but rather the realization that she was still the girl who'd screamed hurtful things at us months before. Her bold statement—*As you can figure, NS (National Socialist) will always be in my views*—meant that nothing had changed. She still held beliefs antithetical to our values. I wanted to give my son a decent, quiet Christmas with none of the drama he'd come to dread. As much as it hurt me to exclude Lauren, after all he'd suffered, I felt he deserved that.

I was relieved when Lauren understood and was pleased to be invited to see her new place. But I awoke to a flooded basement, the result of a quick thaw/freeze cycle that forced three feet of melted snow through unseen cracks in the concrete wall. I frantically called various services and had to stick close to home that afternoon waiting for callbacks. Instead of travelling into Toronto, I invited Lauren and Raymond to Whitby for dinner.

Words can't describe how loathsome I found Raymond. He was polite enough when introduced, but his eyes were cold, he didn't smile and the way he scanned the restaurant gave the impression it wasn't up to his standards. His shorn hair, combat boots and camouflage clothing made me uneasy, and he wore his jacket like armour. There was an eerie feeling of veiled violence surrounding him, as if he were poised to fight with the slightest provocation. Lauren, I thought, you can do better.

Lauren's thick brown hair had, thankfully, recovered from the undercut style she'd adopted when she first landed in Toronto. Now it hung down her back, slightly greasy but long enough to cover the 1488 tattoo on her neck. Eyebrows over-plucked to the thinnest line, blue eyeshadow carefully applied, nicotine-stained fingers, grey and black camouflage pants all proclaimed her a rebel but her smile still contained remnants of the child I remembered, giving me a tiny glimmer of hope.

The family restaurant was half full and I felt as if every eye in the place was on us as we sat down. The hostess and waitress were pleasant but wary; several patrons nearby glanced quickly towards us then studied their menus as if for the first time. Throughout dinner Lauren talked about her life while Raymond remained closed-mouthed for the most part, speaking only to agree or disagree with something she'd said.

"Work's fun," she enthused. "We all whip each other with towels when the diner's closed."

"I'm glad you like your job," I commented. "What's your apartment like?"

"It's small but nice. Came furnished. And the building is decently kept."

"Raymond," I ventured, "what do you do?"

"I'm in roofing," he replied. That was it.

Something in the way she looked at him as he spoke had my gut screaming. He clearly had her under his thumb. I was afraid that if pushed, he could—or already had—become abusive, but Lauren was heading for nineteen, excited about living on her own in a real apartment and no longer open to a mother's protection. At least it was not Donny. Maybe this was a step in the right direction. Maybe she would see what a waste of time her movement was. Maybe, maybe, maybe . . .

I was relieved when Lauren emailed to say that she and Raymond had broken up and that she was at Covenant House. It was reassuring to know she had someplace relatively safe to sleep at night, a place where she could get a few decent meals and a shower. I could have rented her a small place of her own, forwarded money for food and bills, and worried (needlessly) that shelter staff would evict her if they found out that I could afford to provide for her. Was I being a rotten parent? My inner voice told me she needed to experience life for herself and that jumping in to help wasn't going to teach her anything.

I didn't know if she was still hanging out with a white power crew and I was afraid to bring up the topic. I didn't want to hear that she still preferred them to us, that her ideologies hadn't changed, that the chances of my daughter coming home to live with me were slim to none. Lauren had always made a point of telling me they had each other's backs, that they were family, leading me to believe they cared for and respected one another, sticking together against a society they abhorred. Us against them. One for all and all for one. Perhaps that was why she didn't tell me they'd put her in the hospital. Perhaps it was because I didn't ask.

We'd established a tenuous connection, the beginnings of a new relationship based on who we were at that moment. Bringing white power into our conversation, I reasoned, might break the ease with which Lauren spoke to me. Instead, I listened to her tales of the other residents, the staff and the issues she faced when others learned of her involvement in the movement. I hoped she was safe, that she had protection from an angry world and, most of all, that she'd found that sense of community she'd longed for.

CHAPTER EIGHT

Hey, Nazi

LAUREN _____

Thanks to Isabelle, Raymond and Brianna, rumours were circulating that I'd turned Antifa—anti-fascist, the total opposite of white power—so I decided to get my left calf tattooed with Odin's Rune, a mythological Norse symbol the movement had appropriated for its own use. Odin's Runes are symbols of the most powerful forces in the cosmos used by the Norse and Germanic peoples before they adopted the Latin alphabet. When Odin, considered by white power as the "father of the gods," accessed the runes, he was uncovering a very potent form of magic. Odinism, a fairly recent religious sect of white power, values European culture and presumes, just as Hitler did, that "white is right."

Along with Odin's Rune, I added Our Race Is Our Nation, referring to our wish to return Canada to a homogenous community. I wanted to reaffirm, to prove to myself and everyone else that I was still in the movement even though I wasn't part of a crew, because deep down, under my white power mask, I was starting to have some doubts.

While white power crew members proudly claimed to have each other's backs, I had seen more fighting between members than against anyone or anything else, mostly when they'd had too much to drink or done weed, coke or ecstasy behind closed doors. Guys would fight over girls, ripping apart the competition by saying, "He doesn't deserve those tattoos or his position in our movement." They were always trying to discredit each other, jockeying for position within their crews, constantly looking for the ego boost of being a leader.

The women weren't much better—petty and jealous, most of them involved because they were dating a white power guy, they'd spread nasty rumours about each other, like the high school soap operas I remember hearing about.

There were at least five different white power groups operating in and around Toronto during this time. Raymond's crew had been loosely connected to Blood & Honour, a west coast white power organization he'd joined after meeting some of the members online and in person. I'd met a girl online from St. Catherines who belonged to Aryan Nations, knew two guys from Combat 18 (C-18) whom I'd met through Donny, another guy who lived in Bowmanville who was part of the World Church of the Creator and, of course, everyone knew of the Vinland Hammerskins—probably the biggest group in the city.

Members from different groups weren't friendly with one another. Most of us believed the same shit but we didn't get along, often yelling "You're not the real deal" or "You make us look bad" so we had an excuse to fight. We all fed off the same negativity which usually resulted in dick-measuring contests where we'd try to out-fight or out-yell the other side. Members would sometimes leave one affiliation for another, lured by promises of better organization or better parties, so there were fights over that too. Some days it just seemed like a lot of crap.

My goal was self-preservation, my aim to live life minute by minute. I didn't bother looking for meaningful work—my goal each morning was to find alcohol that I could afford with the allowance the shelter provided. Since booze wasn't allowed inside, I drank outside, usually at a nearby park. Some days I'd strike up a conversation with whoever happened to be there; other days, if I drank enough, I'd spend the time in a stupor, unable to recall the following day what I'd done.

Covenant House was a welcome break from the movement's drama, although I tried to recruit some people who didn't feel comfortable there. I had three friends who weren't white power, but many of the other residents harassed me about my neck tattoo. They'd say things like, "Hey, Nazi" and "Hey, 1488, what's it mean?" I tried really hard to ignore their verbal taunting, which became a daily event. It wasn't that I regretted getting my tattoo, although perhaps its placement wasn't well thought-out, but I didn't like being bothered about it, questioned all the time. I was finding other people really annoying.

There was one girl in particular who got on my nerves. One morning, when my friends weren't around, I was feeling annoyed about having such a visible tattoo, ticked off about the beating I'd taken and tired of my life in general, she walked up to me.

"White trash," she spat out.

I stared for a second before throwing a glass of water at her. The staff split us up before we could get into a fight. We were warned not to speak to one another, but the following day, when we ended up together in the outdoor courtyard, there was more name-calling and bullshit. I got mad and threw a chair at her and, after tossing it aside, she demanded, "Why do you have to be like this?"

"Keep your fucking mouth shut and I won't have to be," I told her.

She was soon replaced by an idiot named Mark who tried to get me kicked out by blabbing the meaning of my tattoo to the staff, who, up until then, hadn't asked me much about it. I was told, "Cover the tattoo or you'll be discharged," so I started wearing a bandana around my neck while inside, taking it off only when I left the shelter. Soon after, I saw Mark pasting an image of a swastika on one of the computers in the main lounge area, hoping the staff would blame me. I walked over and grabbed his chair, tossing him to the floor. Neither of us got kicked out, and I enjoyed hearing the other residents laugh at him. I'd heard nobody really liked him anyway.

A new girl named Katy appeared at the shelter following an argument with her parents. She introduced herself to me in the common room and we chatted easily. Twenty or twenty-one with glasses and dark hair, she was intelligent and down-to-earth, not a drama queen like most of the girls I'd met. She seemed very confident, at ease in her own skin. For the next few days, we talked constantly while in the common room or outdoor smoking area, mostly about why we were at the shelter and the circumstances that had led to us leaving home. Aside from my cousin Charlee, Katy was the first girl I'd ever felt completely comfortable with. Our arms brushed as we walked around and my neck tingled whenever she accidentally touched me. A week passed before I realized I was thinking of her all the time. Neither of us had ever dated another girl so I was kind of scared when she made the first move, inching closer before putting her hand on mine as we sat side by side in the common room talking about our dating experiences.

"I've had a few good relationships but I've also had some really crappy ones," Katy confided, just before she touched me.

"I thought my exes were pretty good at first, but I figured out pretty quickly that they really weren't," I admitted.

Putting her hand gently on mine, she said, "They don't need to matter anymore."

I felt a shiver run up my arm and worried someone might notice, but no one else in the room seemed interested in us. I wondered where this was going. I'd felt conflicted when I realized I found girls attractive, but my skinhead beliefs didn't allow me to date them. The white power movement was blatantly homophobic, against gays not just because they don't further the white race but also because they felt the gay community was favoured over straight society. I felt like a total hypocrite, concerned that someone would find out and I'd have to give up either Katy or my beliefs. I didn't want to sacrifice either and a constant war raged inside my head—my beliefs said I shouldn't be doing this and yet, when I was with Katy, I rarely thought about the movement. In my room each night, I'd read my journal, an old notebook I'd picked up months before to record propaganda and rhetoric that I'd found interesting. Reading how no one was naturally gay but swung that way for attention, or how Blacks tried to get back at us for slavery reaffirmed my stance on white power and, for those brief moments, helped me refocus. But when I'd see Katy again, all of that perspective would just disappear. Eventually, I heard the other residents talking behind my back. "Isn't she supposed to be against gays? What is she doing dating another girl?" But nobody said anything to my face, so I didn't have to defend myself or my actions.

Katy and I dated for a month before she got into a fight with another girl. The next day the staff told her, "You've got one night. Then you have to leave." That's how it was at shelters—beds were in short supply so once you went against the rules or had another place to stay, someone else would be invited to move in. Everything happened so fast I never found out if she left because of the fight or because she had someplace else to go. We didn't get to say goodbye and I never heard from her again.

In May, I took the train out to Whitby for my nineteenth birthday. I had dinner with my family and got a new cellphone from my mom. A couple of weeks later, my mom emailed me, requesting that I contact Detective McBride, the Durham Region police officer who'd taken over my case from Detective Paisley. I could guess why. It had been almost a year since I'd left home and over eight months since Donny and I had used my mom's charge card at the Future Shop but police workloads didn't allow them time to search for small-time criminals, so the paperwork was being held until they'd established contact with me. I waited a few days before calling him, mostly because I kept forgetting.

"It's Lauren Manning. I was told to call you?"

"Hi, Lauren," he replied. "Do you know why the police are looking for you?"

"Yes, I think so."

"We have video of you using your mother's stolen credit card. You have two options: you can turn yourself in to police or a warrant will be put out for your arrest."

"I'll turn myself in," I said.

"Do you know where Donny is?" he asked.

"Last time I spoke to him he was in Toronto but I haven't talked to him in a while," I answered. "He told me he was moving to British Columbia."

Detective McBride told me he'd call me on June 11 to set up a date and time for us to meet. As arranged, I took the train out to Whitby on Friday, June 19. When Detective McBride and a uniformed cop pulled up to the curb in front of me, he told me I was under arrest, read me my rights and drove me to the police station. I didn't find it weird getting into the police car, probably because I was drunk at the time. Even before leaving home I'd been a drinker, and I'd been drinking steadily every day since moving to Toronto. Now I was drinking morning and night, feeling like I needed it to get through the day.

I was surprised when the uniformed cop said, "Maybe you can tell us all about the skinhead lifestyle while we drive."

Rather than getting pissed off—I was stuck in the car for the fifteen-minute drive—I said, "Okay, what do you want to know?"

"Who do you hate?"

I launched into my sales pitch. "I can't speak for everyone but, personally, I don't hate anyone. I'm proud of my heritage but as a white person I feel like I'm not socially allowed to be proud of it."

Since I was being charged and released instead of arrested, I was taken into an interview room. The room was small with white walls, two comfortable couches, a small dark brown stained table and tile floors. Cell-like, it had no windows. Detective McBride, in a casual shirt and jeans, sat across from me. His demeanour of "let's get this done and get you out of here" made me feel comfortable instead of defensive. Where Detective Paisley's arrogance had pissed me off, Detective McBride gave off a laid-back vibe that I respected. I was willing to tell him what he needed to know but, between my concussion and the alcohol, my memory was pretty hazy.

"I have to advise you that you're being charged with impersonation and forgery in addition to unauthorized use of credit card data, uttering a forged document, possession of property obtained by crime, fraud under $5000 and possession of a stolen credit card," he began. When I nodded, he asked me to look at a picture of myself and Donny standing in the North York Future Shop.

"Yeah," I said, knowing exactly where this was leading. "I know."

"Tell me your story."

"I used to have a problem with drinking. Donny figured he could get information out of me when I was plastered one night. He'd already worked illegal credit card fraud and wanted to get revenge on my mother because he'd called my house looking for me once and my mother had yelled at him. He had the idea in the back of his mind that he wanted to use my mother as part of his work so he wanted to get the information out of me. He used me. I was on a drinking binge when I was doing all of this, I was just an easy target for him. It worked because I was still pissed off at my mom."

"So how did you get your mother's credit card?"

"We went out to Whitby one night and he'd already got the information out of me, where she kept her stuff."

"Like her purse and that?"

"Yeah, I guess he had lock-picked or something because I didn't take my keys with me. I guess he just figured out where all of her stuff was and came back and was like, okay, we can do it up tomorrow. I was drunk when we committed the crime."

"How long before you ended up at Future Shop?"

"I think like the day after."

"Were you there when he got the credit card?"

"No, I was seeing one of my friends in Whitby. I had left and my friend was like, come over and hang out and whatever, talk."

"Did you know Donny was in Whitby?"

"I went to Whitby first.[1] I had a cellphone at the time but I didn't give that number to my mom because we were still fighting, right. And then Donny called and he was like, yeah, I'm on my way out to Whitby so can you guys meet me? I was like, this was just for me and my friend to hang out. He remembered where my house was because him and my mom used to get along before he started being a retard. My friend lives in the same basic area so we were just at his house and then Donny was like, hey I'm gonna go outside for a second. If I'd known he had his lock pick on him, I would have stopped him, because I was sober at the point and just wanted to talk to my friend. But I didn't realize it."

"Is this all in the same day or is this a couple of days earlier?"

"I went to see my friend I believe the night before that and that's when the break-in apparently happened and then the next morning I was thinking, What on earth happened last night? I know I was with my friend and whatever so when we got back to Toronto it was like five or something in the morning and then I crashed out for a bit."

"And then what?"

"And then I started drinking again and then Donny was like, okay, let's go get you a fake ID. I was like, whoa, wait. What? And he was like, yeah, remember the plan. So more talking me into it. So, we go get the fake ID."

"So, you woke up?"

"Yeah, at Yonge and Bloor, because we had sort of crashed out at our hangout spot. We were dead tired and then he was like, come with me, you're getting a fake ID. I was like, I don't really want to get one and then he was like, yeah, don't you remember our plan? So, he refreshed my memory of the plan, got me drunk again and we went

---

[1] There is a discrepancy between what Lauren now remembers and what she said in the interview

there and, from what I remember, up to Yonge and Sheppard and got the stuff with the card."

"What did you get?"

"A laptop and something else but I can't remember."

"What kind of laptop?"

"Wasn't it an Apple or something?"

"Who had the credit card when you went into Future Shop?"

"Donny did. And then he passed it over to me."

"Who signed for it?"

"Obviously I did because Donny can't pass for a woman."

"Do you know where the stuff actually went when you left?"

"Donny sold it to someone but I don't know who. He has a lot of contacts which I don't really want to know about."

"What was your association to Donny?"

"Just friends at the time I guess and me being a minion, if you want to put it that way."

"How many times was Donny at your house in Whitby?"

"Only like three times before him and my mom started not getting along."

"So, he was allowed to be at your house for the first little bit."

"Yeah, before my mom actually got to know him."

"And then at some point your mom told him not to come back."

"'Well,' I told Donny, 'I'm a skinhead. You can talk all the shit you want around me but be respectful around my mother.' He was telling me and my friend Connor a story about how he got his boots and my mom was in the room and I told him, 'What did I just tell you?' And he said, 'What do I care? It's a true story.'"

"What else did he take from your mother's house?"

"Um, I think her wallet, whatever was in there."

"But all you know of is the Future Shop."

"Yup, I'm not sure if he tried using her bank cards and guessing the PIN."

"Why did you have to get fake ID?"

"So that you can use the credit card because it doesn't say my name on it."

"When the guy took the credit card from you, he didn't notice?"

"He asked to see two pieces of identification and I had gotten two pieces. One looked like a driver's licence, the other one was just like a basic provincial ID. It's the same as this *(pointing to ID on the table)* but it is a different photo because I looked different in it and it said Jeanette Manning."

"When you left where did you go?"

"Just back to our hangout spot. Donny had contacted some people and said they wanted to buy it. I'm not sure of the names that he sold it to, he has a lot of criminal friends. I only helped on this one, then said I don't want to do this anymore."

As the interview wound down, I told Detective McBride, "I didn't get any of the money. He never gave me anything."

"How did you get from living at home to where you are now?" the detective asked.

"I got kicked out because my mom didn't like my friends or what I was into," I said. I could almost see him thinking, Yeah, I'll bet. And you've got a drinking problem.

Detective McBride talked with me, chewed me out for smoking but didn't condemn me for my beliefs. He treated me like an adult, though I'm sure he could see the troubled kid underneath my tough exterior. At the end, when we stood up, he suggested I cover my 1488 tattoo.

"It could bring on more trouble than it's worth," he said, then released me with a Promise to Appear. "Sorry we had to meet this way. Good luck." He sounded as though he meant it.

I stayed at Covenant House for another couple of weeks, working when I could at temporary factory jobs and even doing some modelling. I'd been approached by a friend I'd met at the café, someone outside the movement who wanted to be a photographer. He needed a model, liked the way I wore my heavy-handed makeup, thought the hair extensions I wore every day suited me and wanted some head-shots. "Hey, you should consider modelling for me," he suggested one day when we were shooting the shit. "You'd be great at it. And I'll pay you something for your time." I knew everything would be airbrushed and there wouldn't be much of the real me in the finished product so it wasn't a genuine confidence boost, but I did appreciate the few dollars he paid me.

When some of the Covenant House residents complained about my fighting and my racist mindset, the shelter staff gave me the boot. "Those beliefs aren't appreciated here." I was pissed off. This was so typical of mainstream society. They take everyone else's side—this was how us white folks got treated. The whole "society is against us" narrative replayed in my mind as I packed up my stuff and left.

JEANETTE

When Lauren first moved to Covenant House, I decided to let her live the life she'd chosen. Sticking with that decision was easiest for both of us if I didn't ask questions. I knew she was alive, housed and fed but I had no idea how she spent her days, where she got the money for alcohol and the subway. She told me what she wanted me to know via emails and I was careful not to pry, afraid of driving her away again. I hated the idea of visiting her at the shelter and knew she would resent the intrusion, so I welcomed the opportunity to invite her home for her birthday and hoped the cellphone I gave her would encourage her to stay in touch. Unfortunately, she used it to stay in touch with everyone but me, running up the bill every month no matter how often I brought up her usage. We continued to communicate primarily via email, rarely divulging personal information. Lauren had her life and I had mine.

Having Lauren out of the house and knowing she was relatively safe made my day-to-day existence much easier. If you were to ask my son, I'm sure he'd tell you I was nicer to be around, less angry, less hurt and certainly less focused on Lauren. Between my work, his part-time job and twice-weekly baseball games, our weeks were crammed with activities. We even shopped for a new car, with my son's six-foot-plus height factoring into my choice of a Toyota Prius.

That July my son and I flew to Ireland and spent two fabulous weeks touring the countryside while listening to Irish music and staying in small country inns. Shedding my worries, frustrations and pain for that brief time was a welcome relief, an island of calm in the stormy seas of my family's life, something my mother wholeheartedly approved of. She was our rock, willing to listen when I needed to talk, always believing that Lauren would return to us someday.

Detective McBride didn't share the details of Lauren's charge and release interview with me but provided the date for her upcoming court appearance: Monday, August 10, 2009. I was relieved when he told me it would be a quick appearance and nothing I needed to be present for. The last thing I wanted was to see my daughter in front of a judge, even though I'd been the one to press charges. When the day came, I was tense, unable to focus on work until he called to tell me she hadn't shown up. "In addition to today's charges, your daughter will now face charges of failure to attend court." She had, he went on to say, also failed to appear for her fingerprint and photograph session.

I wasn't surprised but I was angry. She'd been given yet another chance to straighten herself out, to right the wrongs, and once again, it seemed that she couldn't be bothered. Disappointed, disheartened and upset, I wondered for the umpteenth time what life would have been like if Paul had lived.

On August 21, Detective McBride requested that the Toronto Police Services visit Lauren at the address she'd given him, the one for Covenant House, to confirm her residence and to arrest her for failing to appear. The staff told them she hadn't lived there since July 1, when she'd been asked to leave. In direct violation of her previous release conditions, she had failed to notify the Durham Police that she'd left Covenant House and so would now face another charge—breach of bail. When he reached Lauren on the cellphone I had given her, she seemed unconcerned. "I lost my release papers. And I forgot the court date."

More excuses to avoid growing up and being responsible for herself, I thought. That seemed to me to sum up the whole white power life she'd led up until then—evading responsibility, drinking, doing nothing to help herself and not paying a cent towards a society that, while it protected and housed her, also enabled her. Lauren thought of herself as an independent thinker, capable of looking after herself, making her own decisions and running her own life, while in reality she was quite suggestible and easily led, her eagerness to belong, to be part of something bigger a magnet for those willing to exploit her.

When was she going to grow up?

CHAPTER TEN

Hammerskins

LAUREN_____

From Covenant House, I moved to Second Base, a shelter in suburban Scarborough where I found myself uncomfortably in the minority—out of maybe twenty or twenty-five kids staying there, only three of us were white. This is just a place to stay, I told myself from the first minute I stepped inside the door, a bed and a roof over my head, nothing more. I'd better keep to myself.

I was still pissed off about the whole thing with Covenant House and didn't want to get involved with any of the other residents again. I stayed at the shelter for a few months and, since I wasn't working, what little savings I had went pretty quickly on booze and cigarettes. I was looking for a quick fix to my life and alcohol was the easy solution. Maybe I was masking depression with booze or maybe I just wasn't ready to change my circumstances.

One day I received a Facebook message from Ronan, one of the Vinland Hammerskin members I'd met at a Paul Fromm meeting when I was still dating Raymond, inviting me to see Kremator, a hard rock band that was made up of some of their members. *I've never had any issues with you—just your ex. If you can come out, that'd be great.* They were performing in the west end of Toronto.

I spent my last twenty dollars on transportation and arrived at the concert venue to find everyone buying rounds of beer. I wore the boots I had splurged on at a discount place, replacements for those I'd lost to Raymond's crew, and suspenders, all of my tattoos clearly visible. By this time I had six—1488 on my neck, my father's signature on my arm (I'd gotten that one a few months after moving back to Toronto, to remind me that someone had loved me), Odin's rune and "our race is our nation" on my leg, a Celtic cross on my shoulder and RAHOWA (this stood for both "Racial Holy Wars" and the white power band of the same name) on my upper back. I was pleased when Dillon, who I'd kept in touch with on and off, came up to me, gave me a hug and said, "Nice to see you again."

"Hey, nice to see you too."

"Glad you've come over to our side. You'll like us better," he joked.

Looking like someone involved in the movement, I fit in easily and was welcomed by the guys, who could see I shared their beliefs. Few girls went to these shows and those who did rarely looked the part of a skinhead, so I didn't have to worry about getting drinks for myself— not that I had the cash anyway. Some of the guys hinted they wanted to get laid; they thought all the girls went to concerts for that reason alone. Any number of times that night I was encouraged to pick a guy to date but I just wanted to enjoy the music, the booze and partying with people who believed in the cause. I felt buzzed to be included in such a large group that seemed so much more organized than any I'd been with so far. They were more social and being with them revived my interest in and passion for the movement. It also occurred to me that the Hammerskins could provide protection against Raymond and my former crew.

First formed in Texas in 1988, the Hammerskins flirted with the idea of segregation, wanting to build their own community of all-white people and secure the continuation of their race through having children—a practice I didn't personally agree with. They preached traditional family values and were very selective about who was brought into their fold. That meant guys had to look big and menacing, be reasonably articulate when sober but party hard and be able to fight. They should also be holding down good jobs so they'd look respectable. The dress code was one patch only on the guys' jackets, like a uniform, so they'd blend in better. While they tried to appeal to the general public, they were all quite capable of violence. Many of them used steroids and worked out like crazy, maintaining they had to be physically strong to protect "our people." Recruitment was usually achieved through the Stormfront website, the Hammerskins' own site and the promotion and production of white power music, but they'd often poach individuals from street crews, luring them with promises of being "much better organized" than their current groups.

The girls just had to be hot, although I heard that some women involved with the Hammerskins wanted to become teachers so they could teach children to "think for themselves." Apparently, one psychology student was told she should feed white power rhetoric to her future patients as a way of recruiting more people, but she split up with her boyfriend and left the group before she could put that advice into practice. At one time, Stormfront's website even suggested women become librarians so they could replace books with white power pamphlets and literature.

I spent some time that first night talking to Steve, the drummer for the band playing the concert. Tall, thin, with dark hair and a cool goatee, he introduced himself in between sets. We talked about music and when I told him I played bass, some of the other band members overheard and said, "We're interested. It would be good to have a female bassist in the band. Make us look more attractive. Might even attract a bigger audience."

I had a lot to drink and eventually blacked out. Somehow, I woke up in the shelter the next morning but I couldn't remember much from the night before or how I got back into Scarborough. The fact that I could've been in danger didn't occur to me. What was important was the moment, the next drink and my ability to socialize when drunk. Like many in the movement, I used alcohol to help fuel my aggression. I really didn't care what happened to me.

The Hammerskins seemed to like me and I felt pretty special when some of them told me, "You're better looking than most chicks." It wasn't something I'd heard much growing up and, like most women, my sense of identity hinged on how I was perceived and how I felt about my looks. Hearing praise was a lot better than being shamed.

One of the guys, Braedon, had a house in Scarborough where I'd go to party. Through him, I met two Hammerskin guys from British Columbia—Jan and Shawn, both on vacation visiting their Toronto comrades. The first night I met Jan, he told me his mom and stepfather were alive but that he'd left home as a teenager, later travelling to Germany to connect with his birth father. That hadn't gone so well.

"My father didn't give a shit about me. He didn't care whether I was there or not," he confessed, telling me how angry he'd been afterwards. "There was a skinhead group near his house that I hung out with. When I got back to Canada, I looked for another group of skinheads. I wanted to be with people who'd make me feel important, fill the void my father had left. I needed a cause to attach my anger to." Like most of us, the Hammerskins became his family.

Jan and I got along right off the bat. I could have sworn I'd known him forever—he felt like a long-lost friend. He was probably twenty-three at the time, about four years older than me, extremely tall, well-built but very gentle around me. Unlike most of the guys, he wore Adidas sneakers, T-shirts that showed off his muscled arms, and cargo shorts, his brown hair short, his attractive face clean-shaven. I remember telling him I wanted to get into woodworking and instead of telling me that it wasn't woman's work, like the other guys did, he said, "Oh, cool. I hope you can get into that."

Jan had a soft spot for me. He was different with me, funny, his voice gentle and soft. When we'd see each other, he'd gravitate to me, often spending more time with me than with the guys, but no one seemed bothered by it. When he got really drunk, he'd either become violent or really emotional, opening up and sharing almost too much of himself. A few times he had to stop and consider what he wanted to say, especially in front of the guys.

One time he asked me, "Who brought you into the movement?"

"Donny," I said.

"I met him in BC," he mused. "Me and some of the guys there couldn't take his shit so we beat him up."

I laughed. Not many people liked Donny.

Our conversations were rarely about white power. Jan was fun to talk to and interested in me, in my hobbies and what I liked, but there were never any romantic feelings between us. He was respectful, never trying anything during the two weeks he and Shawn were here. I was sad when they returned to BC but he and I were able to stay in contact through email and Facebook. We remained good friends.

I spent the rest of that summer at Second Base, partying mostly, working when I could find temporary jobs, often through Evergreen, a drop-in centre for homeless kids that served meals and helped them find work. While I was there checking out jobs one day, Isabelle walked up to me. At first, I didn't recognize her—she was alone, had grown out her shaved hair, lost the skinhead boots and become really thin—but when I finally clued in that it was her, what stood out most was the shame on her face.

I didn't know what to say to her and remained wary as we stood staring at each other; memories of my beating were still fresh and painful. She didn't say anything but it didn't seem like she wanted to fight. I was stunned when she came closer and said, "I'm sorry."

"For what?" I asked. She was by herself so I wasn't worried about getting ambushed but I still felt guarded, uncertain.

"For the way I treated you last year after you and Raymond broke up."

My mind went blank. What should I say? Surprisingly, I didn't feel any anger or bitterness towards her, so I asked, "What's going on?"

"Raymond and I broke up the other day. You told me he was abusive and manipulative, and I can see that now. He tried to choke me."

Looking into Isabelle's eyes, I was thinking, I told you so. But no one ever wants to listen when they have a crush on someone. While Raymond had never hurt me physically, he'd threatened me more than once during our time together. What I'd suffered had been more mental abuse than anything else. Still feeling somewhat guarded, I stepped forward, hugged her and said, "I forgive you. Just don't do it again."

Not long after, Bentley started messaging me online, saying basically the same stuff Isabelle had said—that he was sorry. I didn't respond at first, mostly because I didn't know what to say. My impression was that he'd set up the ambush, or that he'd been used to get me where they wanted me. Eventually, I called him. "About that message. What's up?"

He talked nonstop, telling me how he'd been arrested at work, how embarrassing it had been, how sorry he was. He didn't seem to want to blame me for any of it, but asked, "Are you still white power?"

I knew he was asking because of the rumours Raymond, Isabelle and Brianna had circulated of my turning Antifa. "Yeah," I answered, ready to forgive him but aware of how little Bentley liked my new crew. "I hang out with the Hammerskins now."

Detective McBride from the Durham Regional Police called me. "I know you didn't have the funds to come out for your court appearance. Unfortunately, we have to put out a warrant for your arrest."

I'd remembered the date but had forgotten the address and lost the sheet of paper listing all the details, so I didn't make it to court. My life was already fucked up, so who cared if I didn't show up? It was just one more thing—in addition to living on the streets, having no place to call home and no family to belong to—that I couldn't bring myself to care about. My thought process had always been more or less "ignore it and it'll go away." And anyway, someone had told me the police didn't actively go looking for people like me, because they're busy with more serious cases, so I felt pretty safe.

I still hung out at the internet café most days. It didn't cost me anything to sit there and I was allowed to use the internet for free because I had no job and no income. I stayed online for hours at a time, usually writing articles and comments on Stormfront's website. One day a guy came over, introducing himself as Shane. "Do you have any weed?"

"No, man," I replied, "I don't smoke that."

"Okay, sorry."

"It's okay," I shrugged. "Whatever."

The second time he approached me, that same day, he said, "I noticed your neck tattoo. I want to get one with a barcode and silhouette of the CN Tower incorporated into it. Where do you think I should put it?"

"Put it on your wrist," I answered, thinking that was the only place it would look good. He didn't seem to have any tattoos and I wasn't sure if he was serious about the whole thing, but he was someone to talk to, so I didn't turn away. Even though I had friends, I didn't see them too often—some worked, some lived far from downtown—so I was lonely, in need of company a lot of the time. We went outside for a smoke and the minute he asked what 1488 meant, I knew he wasn't in the movement. I told him and he snickered, then he asked if I had a boyfriend.

"No," I said, "I just got out of a relationship and I'm not looking."

"Well, if you ever are," he told me, "keep me in mind."

It seemed like a weird thing to say. Definitely not a good pickup line from a guy who was so thin he looked malnourished, his face gaunt, his teeth really messed up—from hockey, he told me when I asked—his long, bleached-blond hair unwashed and slicked back.

"Hey," I said, "I'm involved in a debate. Want to learn more about what I'm into?" I showed him the long, heated, online conversation

I'd been having with a girl I'd gone to high school with, someone I remembered as being very self-righteous. She'd commented on one of my posts entitled "Fuck Obama," ranting that no one should believe in the white power ideology. I'd thrown her arguments right back in her face, something I enjoyed doing fairly regularly with anyone who dared challenge me. "You're the worst thing to happen to the white race," I'd tell them. "You're contributing to the destruction of our race. You're race mixers, adding to the white genocide by having babies that aren't pure." Arguing had become my favourite pastime.

Shane read as I wrote and remarked, "A lot of your arguments are actually very true."

Hey, maybe I can get him to go to some events with me, I thought. I wondered if he was just going along to get close to me but, true to my zeal for the movement, I was focused on recruiting him, not dating him.

Over the next few weeks, I noticed Shane looking at white power sites like Stormfront. He asked me to send him some of the music I liked and soon he began giving Black people the stiff-armed salute, yelling "Sieg Heil!" If he wasn't saying racist things, he'd say stupid, juvenile stuff instead. One time he yelled "penis" to the crowd in the café. I liked that he was entertaining, that his sense of humour was like mine, that he could make me laugh.

Shane told me he was on WSIB supplements (Workplace Safety and Insurance Board's program for anyone injured on the job), living between friends' places and the café. He met a few of the white power guys, seemed to like them, came to our parties but never attended any Hammerskin concerts with me. One of my friends, Mike, questioned if Shane was really into the movement. "He doesn't seem to know much about it. Just nods and agrees." Still, no one tossed him out.

We were just friends, but eventually Shane started calling me his girlfriend. I didn't like it, but it was easier to just go along with him as he was hard to get rid of and wouldn't listen to me. And anyway, I was lonely and liked having company, so I stuck with him. We even had sex once but it was boring and I didn't enjoy it. I'd only agreed to cover my sexual confusion, to change myself from being bisexual to heterosexual. Being gay wasn't natural, according to the movement, and I wanted to fit in, to be normal.

One night, Shane and I were walking down Yonge Street when we ran into a friend of his smoking outside the tattoo shop he owned. Shane introduced us and from the start I thought Tim was really nice. "I might want some tattoos in the future."

Tim looked at my combat boots and said, "I can't do anything racist on you but I'll happily do anything else for a lower price. Just because I know you through this guy," he added, motioning to Shane.

At first, we talked about everyday things but when I noticed the astrological symbol for Aquarius tattooed on Tim's arm, we began talking about astrology, something I'd always been into. I felt a connection with him. In spite of the fact that he was covered in tattoos and looked intimidating, he was incredibly gentle and kind. Two weeks after meeting Tim, he tattooed a Gemini symbol on my right wrist. Luckily, he didn't charge me much; I didn't have a lot of spare cash.

One day, Tim asked me about the signature tattooed on my right arm.

"It's my dad's. He died."

"How old were you when he passed?" he asked.

"Sixteen."

"That's far too young. But obviously," he smiled, "he was a good guy for you to tattoo his name on your skin."

"Yeah, he was," I said. Then I hugged him—something I rarely did—and left.

Many times over the next few weeks, as I walked the few blocks from the subway to the café, I saw Tim smoking outside the shop. I always stopped to talk with him, enjoying his company and the connection we shared. He fell somewhere between an older brother and a second dad.

Eventually, Shane got tired of staying at the café and since I'd gotten myself into trouble with some of the Second Base residents—defending my neck tattoo and beliefs—we applied for welfare and decided to rent a small, furnished room around Jarvis and Dundas Streets. Right away Shane started lighting up indoors, saying, "I got a lot of head injuries and concussions when I played hockey. This helps with my headaches."

"Aren't there other treatments?"

"Nope."

I couldn't stand the smell of pot and told him not to smoke inside.

"Fine," he snarled, heading to our neighbour's room. He spent a lot of time there and was usually wasted by the time he returned. Over the next few weeks, I found a lot of empty pill containers in our bathroom, the names on them never his. I didn't want to know where he got them or what had been inside. It was enough to know he would drink, smoke weed and down pills without a thought as to what he was doing to himself.

Eventually, it became painfully obvious that he was another drama queen. He claimed someone was calling and threatening him but I never heard his phone ring, so I don't know how true that was. When we first met, I'd told him about the beating; soon after, he'd told me he was connected with Hell's Angels, that he'd asked them to keep me safe from Raymond, Bentley and Isabelle. I knew for certain that wasn't true, but Shane liked to show off for me. Once he ran naked down the hallway when the cops were searching our building. He routinely watched kids in shackles coming out of the youth courthouse next door and yell "Ha-ha!" from the balcony, even though he knew there was still a warrant out for my arrest.

Then we'd hear the guards say, "See? People are laughing at you." I worried I'd be the one getting laughed at if he didn't keep his mouth shut.

I told Jan about moving in with Shane during one of our online chats. His response was: *It doesn't seem like you have feelings for the guy so why are you with him?* I didn't have an answer so I brushed him off: *We'll see how it goes.* I changed the subject to our shared frustration with the movement—the fighting that seemed more important than spreading the word about continuing the white race. We'd both seen a lot of infighting and drama although most of what I'd seen had taken place in my former crew, not the Hammerskins. I'd told him about the time I'd been jumped: *They hit a girl? That's really cowardly, four on one.* For his part, Jan was tired of people promising one thing but never following through, something that was really common in the movement.

After a short time with the Hammerskins, I decided to let go of the skinbyrd (female skinhead) image I'd created for myself and start conforming to their dress code. I traded in the half-shaved hair, combat boots, suspenders and bomber jacket for skin-tight jeans, knee-high leather boots and layers of carefully applied makeup. The guys in the movement told me it was better for "our women" to dress well as it made the movement look more attractive. On the outside, I managed to pull it off, looking and dressing the part but on the inside, I didn't feel like myself anymore. The Barbie doll look—hair, makeup and the huge amount of money and time it took every day to get ready—wasn't me but I kept at it because it was expected. I wanted to conform, to belong and I knew I'd hear about it from the others if I didn't.

Drinking at one of the member's houses one night, I said I'd fight in any racial holy war. One of the guys turned to me and said, "There's no way in hell you're going to be fighting on the frontlines for the sake of white power. That isn't a woman's role. Women are happier in their natural habitat and anything beyond that is a product of feminism. Damaging to women and the white race." I knew the Hammerskins believed that feminism "encourages women to leave their husbands, kill their children, practice witchcraft and become lesbians." I'd said similar things myself, partly so I'd get more respect from the guys and partly because I'd never gotten along well with other women. But I had hoped they would make an exception and let me fight since I wasn't a "typical" female.

I was doing odd jobs for cash when I got into the Evergreen youth program, which provided job placement sessions after two weeks of school and life skills. I did well with the courses and told them I wanted to go into construction. They decided to put me in daycare instead. After three days, I couldn't take the whiny kids anymore and quit. "I told you I don't like kids. You didn't listen." They chewed me out and refused to help, so I went back to working odd jobs to pay for my food and alcohol, relying on Shane, who received our combined welfare cheques, to pay the rent and bills.

As Shane liked hanging out by himself, I took to leaving him on his own and often helped Tim clean up the tattoo shop at the end of the day. It was a good excuse to see him, to talk with him. One afternoon I noticed a picture of a Black woman and a child on the wall. "That's my ex-wife and daughter. She took my child away. I haven't seen her since."

My mind provided an instant racial slur. But when I remembered Tim wasn't part of the movement, I was able to put aside my teachings to get past his being married to a Black. I knew if I tried to get into white power stuff with him, it might ruin our friendship.

It was apparent that Tim was trying to numb his pain by convincing himself he didn't need his wife anymore but, because he wouldn't talk about his child, I knew he missed her, that her absence was a sore spot inside him. When he spoke about his ex, he said, "There are some people you don't need in your life anymore."

I felt his words hit home. Regina was one of those people. For the first time I realized that it wasn't worth my time hating her; I could just not care instead.

My relationship with Tim represented a life outside of white power, a break from the everyday boredom and restriction I was feeling. Within the movement, conversations were stale, unoriginal and over-done, the same day in and day out, with no desire for change, whereas my conversations with Tim were interesting, fresh and challenging in a good way. With him, I wasn't repeating the rehearsed speeches I'd been spouting for almost two years. He never tried to dissuade me from being white power, choosing to see the person I was instead. He seemed to enjoy my company and was one of the only people I felt comfortable disclosing my personal life to. Being with him was freeing.

After a while, I realized Shane was spending most of our combined welfare cheque on drugs and booze for himself. I tried to break up with him but, as usual, he talked around my reasoning and made me feel like I was in the wrong. Arguing with him was exhausting. Fuck it, it's too much work, I told myself. Our money was running out and Shane wanted to ask my mom for help, but I held back. We had gone to Whitby a few times to visit her and my brother, but I was afraid she'd hold it over me if she lent me money. When she called one night to ask what was going on, I realized Shane had been sponging off her without my knowledge.

We discussed going back to Whitby, an idea that wasn't as scary as it might have been six months before. The fights I'd had with my mom before I'd left home were still in my head and the thought of going back to that after having built a new, tenuous relationship with her worried me. Conflict was very draining, but I was tired of living on the streets, not having enough money for alcohol, food and rent. It seemed like the best option and we figured the worst answer we could get would be no.

On October 29, 2009, the day before Shane and I left Toronto, I went to see Tim to get his email and phone number, so we could stay in touch. I wasn't sure how long I'd be at home this time but he wished me well, saying, "Hopefully it works out."

JEANETTE

Our lives had been turned upside down by Lauren's affiliation with white power. While she'd lived at home, we'd been hostage to her moods, her rage, her disdain for our values and family. By the time she got involved with Shane, she'd thawed considerably towards us but made it clear she was still happier with her new friends, content to live from welfare cheque to welfare cheque while drinking herself into a stupor on a daily basis.

We first met Shane in our dentist's waiting room. Thinking Lauren's oral hygiene had probably been neglected, I'd scheduled both kids for check-ups and pushed her to meet us at his north Toronto office, which was conveniently close to the subway system. Lauren was wearing an unfamiliar puffy black coat, even though it was summer. Shane wore a nondescript cloth jacket; I wondered if he'd washed his hair that week or brushed his terribly crooked, overlapping teeth recently. I couldn't tell if the strange odour accompanying them was due to unwashed clothing or unwashed bodies—his, hers or both. "Nice to meet you," I said when Lauren introduced us, to which he replied, "Hey."

He's got to be her bodyguard, her protection, I told myself, thinking, She couldn't possibly be attracted to him. There was no spark between them, nothing to say they were anything other than friends, but Lauren seemed comfortable in his presence so I relaxed enough to invite them to dinner at the nearby Moxie's Restaurant once the appointments were over. Shane didn't add much to the conversation but seemed happy to wolf down his food as if he hadn't eaten in days. Unlike Raymond's barely leashed violence or Donny's vibrating tension, Shane's presence seemed underwhelming and big-brotherly, his woe-is-me tone slightly annoying. Another bum, I concluded. She's hooked up with yet another scumbag who's out to use her. When would my daughter stop settling for the bottom of the barrel? Why did she feel she could only attract these types of men?

Whereas months before Lauren had spouted racist rhetoric or bragged about handing out flyers to unsuspecting immigrants, she now shared antics and funny stories of the people she'd met, her attitude calmer and friendlier than I'd expected. I found myself enjoying our dinner. One look at my son confirmed that he too was surprised—pleasantly. Still, it was all I could do not to gag on the stench coming from the coats they'd hung on the back of the booth.

In September, Lauren brought Shane and a casual friend named Sidney home for dinner. My impression of Shane hadn't changed; he seemed more bodyguard than boyfriend and I felt somewhat relieved knowing she was being looked after. Sidney was a nasty little welfare cheat who blatantly told me he expected the middle class to support him while he derided our way of life, whining that the government wouldn't give him disability for being gay. Visions of running him down with the lawnmower danced through my head as he spoke.

We talked comfortably, as if Lauren had been living with us the whole time. In spite of her now bleached blond hair and tattoos, her unattractive clothes and pervasive body odour, I was happy to see her eat a good meal. She'd settled down and not everything she said pertained to white power or racism. In fact, I remember us joking and laughing over dinner, reminiscing about her childhood antics.

When it came time to drop them at the train station, I felt an ache inside me but was resigned to our circumstances, to the knowledge that Lauren was now an adult and somewhat responsible for herself. She was happy. But seeing her with people I'd considered losers who wouldn't work to support themselves helped me understand some aspects of her personality that hadn't been apparent before. I'd always thought of her as one who led others into trouble, someone who attracted trouble, but now I saw her as more of a follower, content to bask in the company of anyone who paid her scant attention. First Donny, then Brodie, Raymond and now Shane—men who used her for what she could give, be it money for rent and booze or social stature for having a pretty girl at their side. Her appearance, something she'd struggled with most of her life, was now dictated by those friends whose bullshit she swallowed without question. I saw that Lauren attracted two kinds of people—losers with agendas and birds with broken wings, those who needed parenting themselves.

We may have felt more at ease with each other, but Lauren was still keeping secrets from me, still only telling me what she wanted me to know. I often wondered where she got the money for tattoos and alcohol when she rarely had any in her pockets. So it didn't surprise me when Shane called me that fall, asking for rent money to cover the following two weeks. He'd confided, "Lauren doesn't know I'm asking you. She didn't want to have to take money from you."

"What happened to your funds?" I asked. "I thought you were both getting welfare."

"The landlord raised the rent," he lied smoothly. "Lauren and I can't afford next week's but she's got a line on a job so we should be okay after this."

I naively believed I was helping my daughter. She'd always been proud so I knew she wouldn't ask for help. I wanted her to stand on her own two feet but what harm could it do to help them out? Just this once. I arranged to send Shane the money.

When he called a second time—"We're short on this week's rent. Welfare doesn't pay enough to cover this place"—I told him to put Lauren on the phone.

"What's going on? I thought you used the money I sent to pay your rent."

"I never got any money," she said. "But the landlord's going to evict us for not paying last week's rent. So if you could . . . "

"Where did the money go?' I persisted.

"I don't know," she replied hesitantly. "But Shane's been doing a lot of drugs lately, using our combined welfare cheque for his shit."

"Why does he have your welfare money?"

"They put both under his name. Dunno why but that's what they do all the time. They call it a couple's cheque."

"If I send this to you, it's for the rent. Got it? Nothing else."

"Yeah," she said quietly. "Thanks."

This time, I sent the money to Lauren.

I couldn't ignore her situation any longer. They had both sponged off taxpayers for long enough, relying on the welfare system when she was perfectly able to hold down a job. It was just wrong, so when we spoke later that week, I offered both of them a place at home, on two conditions: that Lauren turn herself in once she arrived in Whitby and that both of them get jobs or go to school. I hoped that, by allowing them to live rent-free, they'd get their act together and become the adults they were, and that Lauren would realize she belonged with us, not with Shane and not with the movement. Although neither of us brought up past "rules of the house," I think we both understood things would have to change for it to work this time.

CHAPTER ELEVEN

Justice

LAUREN_____

My mother offered Shane and me a place at home on two conditions: that I turn myself in to the police and that we both get jobs or go to school. I knew I'd have to talk to the police at some point anyway, and even though I didn't think I was ready for college, I figured I'd give school a shot. The day before Halloween 2009, my mom met us at the train station. As soon as we got home, she gave me the phone and said, "Make the call."

I asked for Detective McBride. "I'm back in Whitby and I'll turn myself in, in the morning."

Later that evening, Shane and I went grocery shopping with my mom. Five minutes after we got home, Detective McBride, his partner and two uniformed officers rang the doorbell. I wasn't really surprised that he'd shown up earlier than we'd agreed. Standing in the doorway, his plainclothed body blocking my view of the street, he said, "We're going to take you in tonight. That way the judge will start on your case tomorrow and you'll be out faster, alright?"

He instructed me, right there in the front hallway, to remove my piercings, my jewellery and the drawstrings from my hoodie. Then he escorted me outside, walked me to the waiting car and helped me inside, where he handcuffed me. I was great at numbing my feelings, so it was no big deal for me to be taken away by the cops, in front of the whole neighbourhood.

I was taken to 17 Division in downtown Oshawa, about ten minutes east of us. The female officer doing intake naturally questioned me about my tattoos. "So, you in a skinhead gang or something?"

When I'd first joined the white power movement, another member had lectured me on how to act in front of cops and in jail. "Just say, 'I have nothing to say,' or 'I'm in a political movement, not some lame street gang.'" We all knew the movement wasn't well thought of by law enforcement and thought it best to dress up the rhetoric.

"No," I replied. "I'm in a political movement."

She sighed. "It's a gang, Lauren."

Wordlessly, I was escorted into another room for fingerprinting. It was dead silent and the air was cold. The back of my neck tingled and I shivered a bit from a combination of fear and nicotine withdrawal. I shut down mentally and time became a blur. When we were done a male officer walked me down a hallway lined with cells. Stopping before an empty one, he opened the door and said, "All yours. Enjoy yourself." Then he left.

The cell reminded me of the room I'd been in at CAMH, except this one was much darker and dirtier. It was about ten feet by six feet with a small concrete ledge, bare of any covering, for me to sit or lie on. There was also a toilet with no water, no seat and no toilet paper, nothing for me to potentially hurt myself with. The air was stale and cold, like our basement at home. Shadows lurked in the corners where the unpainted walls remained clean of any graffiti.

I'd crashed on park benches and the floor of the café, so sleeping on the cell's concrete ledge wasn't a huge issue. I dozed off a few times until a young woman named Amanda was brought in for drunk driving. I couldn't see her but I had no problem hearing her arguing with the cops. "I only had two glasses of wine," she yelled more than once.

"You blew more than twice the legal limit," they answered. Amanda kept screaming at the guards and banging her head against the wall. She sounded young and naive and some part of me felt bad for her, but I mostly wanted to laugh. I'd behaved a lot better than she had.

For hours the guards warned Amanda, "If you keep screaming and banging your head, we'll put you in a special cell with a restraint chair. It's got handcuffs and a helmet," but she wouldn't listen. One of the officers eventually opened her door and said, "Alright, I warned you. Come with me." Less than a minute later, I heard her scream, the shackles jingling noisily as she was put in the chair. She kept at it for most of the night.

In jail, every minute feels like an hour. Hours feel like days. There's nothing to do, nothing to take your mind off the boredom of four walls. I thought about the stories I'd heard from the guys in the movement—how they'd intimidated and beat other inmates while serving time. I'd been willing to listen then but now started questioning whether that was true. Later, when one of the guards tried to strike up a conversation, I realized how burnt out I was, how emotionally closed off and exhausted I felt. I don't think I was the best person to chat with that night.

When I was finally released on Saturday afternoon, my mom met me at the courthouse. The judge gave me a set of conditions to comply with. "You are to notify Durham Regional Police Services in writing within twenty-four hours in the event that you change addresses," he began. "Furthermore, you are to abstain from communicating and associating directly or indirectly with Donny. You will not possess any identification, credit cards, debit cards, bank cards, cheques or financial documents unless they are legally in your own name and lawfully encoded with corresponding data."

As soon as he stated the next two conditions, I knew they'd been my mom's suggestions. Would she ever stop trying to run my life? "You will pursue and attend education, training or gainful employment. And you will comply with all house rules."

I'd been away from home for more than a year and wasn't sure I *could* follow my mother's rules. I wanted control over my own life and wondered if I'd be able to go back to school. I could easily memorize white power rhetoric the same way I could memorize a favourite song, but I'd never been good at studying or schoolwork. I was worried my mother was going to choose the school for me like she had before and figured getting a job would be difficult because of the tattoo on my neck. Even if people didn't know what it meant, it still looked like I'd gone to prison.

We got home mid-afternoon and I couldn't wait to shower and have a cigarette. Shane didn't meet me at the door, didn't ask how I was. In fact, we pretty much ignored each other for the rest of the day. Fine, whatever, I thought. I told myself I didn't really care. In some ways, I was happy not having to deal with his stupidity. I repressed my feelings as much as I could, reaching out to the guys from the Hammerskins. I texted Steve, the drummer I'd become good friends with, and told him what had happened. We had a good laugh about the whole thing before I texted Jan. He asked me about my visit to jail: *How are you doing after your night in the Grey Bar Motel?*

Okay, nothing cool happened in there except for this broad getting put in the restraint chair. Lol.

Where are you?

Back at home.

I hope it works out well for you.

A few days later, I contacted two high school friends, Marco and Brett, whom I'd kept in touch with online after leaving home. Marco was one of my Grade Eleven drinking buddies, someone who kept his mouth closed and didn't gossip like a lot of the other guys. We got along well, our dirty minds drawing us together. He was one of few people not to judge me. "Whatever you're into, it doesn't change the fact that you're my friend," he'd remind me.

Brett and I had been classmates. I always liked that he talked back to the teachers and could hold an intelligent conversation. We didn't communicate much after I left home, but when we messaged each other, the connection was still real. Now I found out he'd once identified as white power too. He told me he'd turned recently and now called himself an anarchist/libertarian. My knowledge of libertarianism was limited—I'd been taught, "If you're not with us, you're against us"—but Brett always said, "I don't believe in labels," and had practised that by not conforming to any one stereotype.

He suggested getting together so we met up a few blocks from my house. I gave him a hug when I realized he was still my friend, regardless of what he—or I—believed. On our way back to my place he mentioned feeling slightly nervous about hanging out with me at my house. "It's just that I've been set up before."

I turned to him and paused, remembering the months I'd spent trying to regain basic cognitive function after being jumped, then reassured him I had no intention of doing anything like that to him. "No offence taken," I said. "I understand where you're coming from."

Once home, I introduced him to Shane, who didn't even look Brett in the eye when he shook his hand. Later, Brett said, "I don't think Shane likes me very much."

"Yeah," I shrugged, "I'm not sure what's going on with him. We'll hang out by ourselves while Shane does his own thing."

I gave him a tour of the house, and when he saw my room he started laughing.

"What's so funny, dude?"

"Your room is nothing like I expected," he said, "I thought I'd see a giant white pride flag on your wall."

My room looked exactly as it had when I'd left. I hadn't been home long enough to redecorate the bright red and yellow walls, covered with artwork that, I had to admit, I loved more than any white power posters or flags. Right then, Brett could see that I hadn't really changed that much on the inside, even though I wore a racist mask.

We recounted high school stories over a few beers, laughing at the Grade Eleven Psychology debates he'd won and the many times he'd corrected the teacher. "Oh yeah," he said, "I had a huge crush on the teacher."

"Yeah, she was hot," I replied, then felt my face redden. When he didn't say anything, I had to remind myself that I wasn't talking to a bunch of hardened, racist, homophobic dudes. I was relieved when he carried on as if nothing had happened.

I walked Brett part-way home, sad to see him go but happy that our friendship hadn't changed, despite our different beliefs. All the way back, I kept thinking, Man, why the hell did I ever lose touch with him?

When I got home, I asked Shane, "What's going on? You didn't want to hang out with us?"

He just grunted. "I'm trying to adjust to living out here in Butt Fuck Idaho. I don't want to meet all of your friends."

I shrugged it off. "Eh, whatever. Your loss." By then, whatever feelings I might have had for Shane were gone. I was slowly detaching from him.

JEANETTE

I never imagined there'd be a worse feeling than knowing your child was a white supremacist, but I was wrong. I was shaking as I watched the police officer escort Lauren to the unmarked car idling at the curb. Detective McBride knew that Lauren's father had been with the police and, out of respect, did us a favour by arresting Lauren right away, so she wouldn't have a chance to flee, and handcuffing her inside the car, where I wouldn't have to see it. But when the car door closed on her, I fell back against the wall and wept uncontrollably.

My son consoled me, his strength reminiscent of his father's. I'm certain he felt the same shock and shame I did but he hid them well for my sake. He'd been remarkably mature, calm and reassuring throughout the whole ordeal and was as prepared as he could be for her homecoming. Shane, on the other hand, walked away from the scene at our front door as if nothing unusual had happened. He didn't say much, didn't appear worried for his "girlfriend." In fact, he seemed happy just to have a place to stay and food at his disposal. I was livid when he holed up in the spare bedroom, likely playing video games on its small television.

I got the call from the courthouse the next morning, just as I was distracting myself by putting in some overtime at work. "Your daughter's going to be in front of the Justice in an hour." I was relieved to know Lauren had survived the night and hoped the lock-up had scared some sense into her. Maybe, I thought during the short drive, this would be her rock bottom, the start of her journey out of white power and into a decent life.

Since Shane hadn't shown any interest in Lauren's legal problems, I didn't bother picking him up before heading to the courthouse. It was increasingly clear that he and Lauren weren't romantically involved but rather reliant on each other for some other means of support. I wondered how long I was going to have to deal with him before she'd come to her senses and ditch him.

I met with the Justice before Lauren's appearance in front of him. "What conditions would you like to see imposed on your daughter?"

I could only think of the two I had already told Lauren: attending school or work and following house rules. The first, I hoped, would give Lauren something new to focus on while the second would give us an opportunity to hash out rules we could both live with. I wanted peace and calm, a chance to build a new relationship with her. A new future for all of us.

Then he asked me to sign our house over as collateral for Lauren's bail, something I found very difficult to understand.

"Your Honour," I protested, "My daughter's charges stem from ripping me off. You're asking me to sign away my home as surety,

and yet I'm the victim here. Doesn't that seem a bit ironic to you?"
Nevertheless, I signed the papers for Lauren's release and walked her
to the car, exhaustion and nervousness dogging my steps. I hadn't
slept well the night before and, if her grey pallor was any indication,
neither had Lauren. We drove home in tense silence, each of us lost in
our own thoughts.

The court order gave Lauren and me the tools necessary to set
boundaries and limits we could both live with as she tried to re-enter
the world she'd left behind. Several days after her court appearance we
sat down and hashed out our list, which included things like speaking
respectfully to her brother and me and keeping her language clean. We
agreed that she would refrain from discussing her beliefs at home, not
use racial slurs and help with the Sunday cleaning.

My daughter was now legally an adult who had spent more than
a year away from me, looking after herself, foraging for accommo-
dations, decent meals and essentials. I knew our "rules of the house"
had to be flexible so she'd feel comfortable living at home. Unlike
previous attempts, this time I engaged her in the discussion, asking
for her input instead of dictating terms. The court order encouraged
her to participate—she understood that not following it meant she
could wind up in jail again, this time farther away and for longer.
I was pleased when we were able to agree but even so, she made it
clear that her acceptance was conditional. "As long as no one tries to
change my opinions."

CHAPTER TWELVE

Home. Again.

LAUREN _____

Within a week of being home, Shane started acting weird. He'd always watched a lot of horror films, claiming they were based on reality; now he talked about burning the old Ouija board he'd found in the back of my closet, making a big deal of something I'd long since forgotten. I'd often hear him wandering around the house after everyone else had gone to bed and when I confronted him, he said, "I have night terrors."

I had enough problems of my own and wasn't mature enough to help anyone else through their psychological issues. Shane wouldn't listen to me anyway. "I don't really know how I can help," I shrugged.

One night he swore he'd seen flashing lights in the sky. "Come outside. Look—those look just like the lights on a spaceship. I've seen paranormal activity before."

I laughed at him. "What kind of drugs have you been doing? Can I have some?"

He grunted and said, "Lauren, I'm not trying to fuck with you. Why won't you believe me?"

He'd been playing the white power act so, tired of his constant bullshit, I said, "No self-respecting white nationalist would ever believe in alien invasion or smoke whatever you're smoking."

He snarled at me, "Yeah, you and your friends know nothing of what white power is all about."

"We know more than you. You were with a brown girl before I met you."

For the first time, I was seeing just how screwed up he was. And the longer he stayed, the stranger things became.

One night, tired of hearing his claims about an alien invasion, I pulled a prank on him. It was ten o'clock and I could hear Shane pacing in the next room. Grabbing a flashlight, I went outside and walked to his bedroom window where, laughing almost uncontrollably, I shone a light, holding it still for a minute before switching it off and creeping back inside.

The next morning, I woke to him knocking on my door. He barged into my room, his voice frightened. "Something weird happened last night. I was trying to sleep when a bright light came through my window. I think some strange entity is out to get me!"

I managed to control my laughter until he left—but it wasn't easy.

After six weeks, his drug habit was getting out of hand and the tension at home was thick. My mother told me she had seen Shane going into the garage with a bag of what looked like drug paraphernalia. I finally confronted him. "What was in that bag? And what are you doing that I don't know about?"

He avoided the question. "Why don't you ever believe me or take my side?" he asked.

"Because I don't trust you," I told him. "Know what? We're finished."

Once I told my mother the news, she told Shane, "Now that you and Lauren aren't dating, it's time you moved on." She gave him a deadline of noon the following Thursday, the day I'd invited Steve, my drummer friend, to visit. The days dragged. I spent as much time away from him as possible, but when I was at home his stony silences, self-pity and the wasted hours he spent playing video games in his room just pissed me off more. I could see how stressed out my mom was.

"I can barely look at him," she confided one evening as we drove to Markham to visit family friends. "Everything about him creeps me

139

out—the way he skulks around, his lack of manners, his unwilling-
ness to shower—I can't wait for him to leave."

Steve arrived that Thursday around noon, when Shane was supposed to leave, but he sat on the couch in the den, refusing to go.
I tried being polite, saying things like, "There's a bus leaving in ten
minutes," to which he'd reply, "Oh, I'll catch the next one." In my
head I was screaming at him, Would you fucking leave already? All I
wanted was for him to go so I could have a decent conversation with
Steve, but instead he just sat there. Every time he cut me off in conversation, I'd cut him off, getting louder and louder until he shut up.
Steve managed to stay calm, letting me deal with Shane on my own
until, around four o'clock, Shane finally gave up and left. When the
door closed, Steve smiled and said, "Finally, we can enjoy ourselves." I
don't know if Shane would have left if Steve hadn't been there.

That night, when my mom and brother got home, I introduced
them to Steve. He wasn't as cocky as the other guys in the movement,
his tattoos—mostly on his upper arms and shoulders—were hidden
beneath his T-shirts so he wouldn't look so obviously white power at
work. I liked that he wore his Doc Martens and flight jacket easily
and his perverted sense of humour was like mine. My mom seemed to
like him—he had a job in telecommunications, a house, a car and was
respectful to my family and to me. Even if they didn't agree with our
white power beliefs, my mom and brother appreciated the fact that
Steve was polite when he was with them. While the four of us had
dinner together that night my mom told stories of the stupid things
I'd done as a child.

"Lauren used to watch *Beavis and Butthead* religiously and then
do impersonations of them all the time," my mom told Steve.
"Every single morning we'd hear, 'I am Cornholio! I need TP for my
bunghole.'"

Laughing, Steve tried hard not to choke on his dinner. When I
went outside for a cigarette, he joined me, even though he didn't

smoke. We chatted and eventually, when he told me he liked me, I replied, "I'd like to date you." We spent the rest of the evening, until he left around midnight, just talking and sharing stories. It was nice to have an adult conversation for a change.

By the time Christmas came around, I felt happy to have a roof over my head and a nice boyfriend who held the same beliefs as me. I was also getting along pretty well with my mother and brother, something I was grateful for, as I had missed the previous Christmas. The house didn't feel as much like a prison as it had before I'd left; the rules weren't nearly as harsh as those imposed on me after the incident with Casey. I had to laugh when Nana, who'd come for dinner Christmas Eve, told me she was proud of me for telling Shane to shut up the last time she'd joined us for dinner. "I never liked him," she confided.

On Christmas Day we were expected to visit with my dad's family. It was going to be weird as these were people I'd lost contact with because of my racist views. I figured Regina's mother would paint me as the bad guy while an aunt would no doubt be vocal in her opposition to my beliefs. Most of the relatives were in or had been to university; compared to me, fresh from living on the streets and in jail, they were golden. I had no idea how to make conversation with any of them, let alone create a human connection. I didn't want to be part of the family competition, the "beauty contest" I'd experienced before, so I wore faded jeans and a black hoodie and made no effort to cover the 1488 tattoo.

When we arrived at my grandfather's house, a few of my relatives, including my Gramps, hugged me and said, "Merry Christmas. Good to see you again." I was surprised and pleased but still felt like some kind of pariah, spending most of the evening debating whether to try to make conversation or just walk out the front door.

When Regina arrived, she stared at me for a moment as I stared back. My mom had already lectured me on how I should apologize for my part in our falling-out but that wasn't going to happen. Hell no, I thought. I was not apologizing for shit. She wasn't innocent and was just as much to blame for that whole incident as I was. Regina turned away to talk to someone else. My mom tried to get me to talk to her but when I said, "No. Not happening," she let it go.

On the ride home, my mom asked, "Why won't you apologize?"

"Because," I responded, "I am not a pushover. You and I both know she was as much to blame as I was."

My relationship with my brother had improved drastically. We spoke candidly when my mother wasn't around, mostly about music and our relatives and he admitted to seeing many of the same traits that I'd seen. It felt good to know I wasn't the only one who saw through them, who felt uncomfortable. I think my mom felt it important to maintain connections with them for our sakes, because of my dad but, as far as we were concerned, it was mostly wasted time.

That Christmas was weird but I was hoping the new year, 2010, would be better. A few days after New Year's, I reached out to Tim, who'd helped me so many times when I'd been on the streets. I missed him. I knew he'd understand how difficult my transition home had been—and still was—and that he'd be happy to know I finally had a decent place to live.

My call went unanswered, so I left a message. Shortly afterward, I received a call from one of his friends. "Tim committed suicide on New Year's Eve. He was found on New Year's Day."

I was speechless. Tim had been my family while on the streets, my *chosen* family, the friend I could trust with anything. Could I have done something to prevent this? Maybe reached out to him? Not been so preoccupied with my own issues? Thoughts ran through my head, over and over. I could have kept in touch more often. I should have, I told myself angrily, blaming myself more and more, wracked with guilt that I'd missed the signs of his own unhappiness. Why hadn't I spent the holidays with Tim instead of being angry, instead of wasting energy on my relatives? As I grieved for my friend, I began to understand what had driven him to that point: his wife had left him and he'd had no contact with his daughter. His beloved dog, whose picture he'd had tattooed on his arm, had passed away months before. Obviously, in spite of the front he'd worn around me, he'd felt alone, his life too painful to face. He'd felt there was no other way out and nothing to live for.

When I told Steve what had happened, his response wasn't what I'd hoped for. "Sorry to hear that. But people who commit suicide are weak." He was buying into what we'd all been told—if you're going to kill yourself, you might as well take out some of the undesirables as well. I didn't think of suicide like that, maybe because I'd entertained thoughts of it myself and understood what a difficult a choice it was.

Jan had never met Tim but when I told him about his death, he was very supportive: *I'm sorry to hear that. How did it happen?* In fact, I found Jan more caring about Tim's passing and my feelings than Steve. I was really disappointed in Steve's response, but not surprised by Jan's.

For a long time, I wished that phone call had been a bad dream. But it wasn't. When I walked by his shop a month after his death, another tattoo shop was in its place. That's when reality finally hit me. Tim wasn't coming back.

JEANETTE

I was so relieved to have Shane out of my house. From the minute he arrived he'd pissed me off—not bothering to support or spend time with Lauren, not showering, not tidying up after himself. He made the odd token effort, offering to set the table for dinner one night, trying to engage my son in conversations about video games, and showing up half-way through the Christmas decorating smelling like day-old urine. I promptly told him to shower. "But I want to decorate the tree," he whined. "We never had one when I was growing up." I could barely look him in the eye.

My son confided that, "Lauren was telling him how useless he is and he just stood there, taking it."

"What do you think of him?"

"I don't really bother with him, other than shooting the shit. But at least he isn't spewing white power crap like Donny did."

Late one afternoon, Lauren called me at work to say they'd both gone for job interviews in downtown Whitby but they'd taken the bus too far and weren't sure where they were or where they should be. "I'll be there shortly," I said, irritated. "Don't move."

On the ten-minute drive, my anger boiled over. How the hell could they get lost? Why couldn't they do something for themselves for once? And when were they going to grow up, act like adults? Of course, they weren't where they said they'd be. I found them several blocks away, walking towards the store they'd been looking for. "Get in," I yelled.

"But we found the place," Lauren protested weakly.

"I don't give a damn. Your interview was an hour ago—they aren't going to hire people who can't get to the interview on time. Get the fuck in this car, both of you." My language was uncharacteristically coarse, a sign of how angry I was.

I kept up a steady tirade the whole drive home. Shane gave me lame excuses: "I lost the address" and "if we call and apologize maybe they'll interview us." Lauren offered a small apology for making me leave work early to rescue them but the whole incident made me see how little they were trying. Later on, when I'd calmed down, Lauren and I talked about it. She admitted, "Shane doesn't like Whitby. He doesn't want to get a job. He just wants to stay here because it's free."

"Uh, yeah, I kinda guessed that," I said. "I'll give you both one more chance to straighten up and do something with your lives."

Their solution was to register with a private college in Toronto. Shane was supposedly getting welfare money to cover the exorbitant fees for a two-year course in video game design. Lauren chose interior design and would use the money her dad and I had set aside for education. "Why did you choose interior design?" I asked her. In my college days, only moneyed, blond-haired socialites took those courses. I couldn't see how she'd fit in.

"Well, um," she stammered, "It was the only course that sounded interesting. Shane and I wanted to go to the same place and that's where his course is."

Lauren and I visited the college, toured the building and purchased hundreds of dollars worth of supplies, sharing a laugh over a mother who complained, "They don't take Amex." Shane, meanwhile, languished at home. "I'll get my stuff when school starts." Of course, that day never came because he hadn't bothered to enrol. It was just lip-service, intended to shut me up while he enjoyed free room and board.

It was a huge relief to tell Shane he'd have to leave after Lauren broke up with him. I chose the day of Steve's visit as Shane's last day so that Lauren would have protection if Shane tried something or became difficult. I thought he'd be less likely to make a scene with someone else around.

Steve, on the other hand, seemed like a mother's dream—he worked full-time in an office, owned his own car and house, was nice, clean, kind to my son and respectful of Lauren. He might have shared her white power beliefs but he didn't discuss them in our home. I had hopes that, fourteen years older than Lauren and close to his own family, he would help her adjust to life at home, that he'd provide a stable relationship so she wouldn't go back to the dregs she'd dated before. Steve also fulfilled a big brother role for my son; the two of them comfortably talked sports, movies, music and video games. For that, I was grateful to have him in our family. It was easy for me to forget that both of them still believed in white power, easy to ignore the fact that their friends were Hammerskins. When they were at our house, they acted like any ordinary couple. White power was never discussed, one of the rules I'd insisted upon.

As the year drew to a close, I was grateful my child was back at home, with us, where she belonged and that she and her brother were able to reconnect. It hadn't happened overnight. My son was wary of Lauren's motives for being at home, worried he'd have to hear racist rhetoric or be witness to more arguments. But they were gradually able to establish a relationship that included honesty and openness and the closeness they'd known as youngsters.

I hoped Lauren would apologize to Regina to ease the tension I knew we'd experience on Christmas Day. I wanted us to fit in, to be part of what I saw as their perfect Brady Bunch existence. We had never been close and, without a good foundation to build upon, the support promised after Paul's death had never really materialized despite efforts on all sides. But I persisted, determined to give my children the perceived stability I'd missed in my own life.

Even though I'd never admitted how deeply involved in white power Lauren had become, word had gotten out and her reception was cool, to say the least. I knew it would take more than an apology for any of them to accept her into their circle again. And she wasn't even ready for that. It occurred to me that I was forcing my kids into situations both uncomfortable and awkward, trying to make both them and myself into something we weren't, so I could feel as though I belonged somewhere. Maybe I wasn't so different from Lauren after all.

CHAPTER THIRTEEN

Intermission

LAUREN

I started my interior design course at a small, private school in Toronto in January and soon realized it wasn't a good fit for me. My classes were comprised of upper-class girls whose parents had more than enough money for private college and who looked down their noses at me. For the most part, I'd stopped dressing white power when I'd moved home, but my teacher still criticized my jeans and dress shirt, "You need to dress more lady-like. Get that tattoo off the side of your neck." I couldn't make it through one presentation without saying "fuck"—it was programmed into my speech patterns—which also didn't make a good impression. But at least I didn't feel the same sense of not belonging that I had in high school, primarily because I didn't like many of my classmates. I lost interest very soon after my first week and ended up dropping out after the first semester.

Eventually, the date of my sentencing hearing arrived. My mother and I met my lawyer, a really cool guy who'd been assigned by Legal Aid, at the courthouse in Oshawa. He and I had spoken a few times before; I liked him because he told me he'd lost his mother when he was young, so he knew how it felt to lose a parent.

The day started with the prosecutor, a woman in her late thirties, ranting about something before court was even in session. My mother said, "She's not in a great mood today. You may be in for some trouble."

When it was my turn, the prosecutor spent more time criticizing my involvement in white power than she did speaking about my case.

"It was stated in the pre-sentence report," she said forcefully, "that Ms. Manning is part of a white supremacist gang in Toronto." I had tried to omit my involvement in the movement from the pre-sentencing report but, when they'd interviewed my mom, she'd dropped that information and the fact that I'd been self-harming after my dad's passing.

The prosecutor continued. "This kind of antisocial behaviour is a threat to the public and it's my belief that a harsher penalty is of benefit to the public. I realize a conditional discharge is in her best interest, Your Honour, but it's in the public's best interests to sentence her to a higher degree. It's my hope that, since she comes from a loving family, she will leave this hatred, racism and violence behind her and learn to look beyond a person's skin colour."

Lady, if you'd known our family a couple of years ago you wouldn't have thought we were functional, much less loving, I thought as I listened to her. I couldn't help but remember the fights we'd had, the arguments about my friends and the time I was spending on the computer, and the months I'd wasted waiting for my "online boyfriend."

My lawyer glossed smoothly over my involvement in the movement and ended by saying, "Lauren's made mistakes but she's planning to go back to college in the fall. In my opinion she'll be a success someday."

I was surprised when the judge called me to the stand, asking if there was anything I wanted to add. "Not really," I said.

He launched into a speech about the life of crime I'd chosen. "I understand your father passed away before you joined the movement. It isn't an easy thing for anyone to go through. However, I don't think your father would be very proud of your choices up till now."

I always hated hearing, "What would your father think?" It was guilt-tripping and all it did was make me want to act out more. I denied up and down that my dad's passing had anything to do with my subscribing to white power ideology. I felt as though admitting to that would have left me without my shield and given the judge other opportunities to tear me down. Don't show any vulnerability; they'll take advantage of it just like all our enemies do, I told myself. Don't argue—these people are manipulative and they'll mind-fuck you if they can.

When he continued to use the word "hate" I interrupted him. "The movement isn't about hate, it's about pride. I am entitled to my opinion and I have never beaten up anyone who isn't white," which was true. My scraps had been with other group members and white kids I'd tangled with in shelters and on the streets.

Nothing I said seemed to matter. But the judge was decent and respectful, speaking to me as an adult rather than a stupid, naive little girl. I think having my mother there helped with both the prosecutor and the judge, who ended up siding with my lawyer. I received a lesser penalty: along with my existing bail conditions, I was to perform one hundred hours of community service and attend drug and alcohol education classes.

Later that night, I was chatting online over Messenger with a Facebook friend who was in the movement in Norway. When I told him what had been said in court he replied: *Oh yeah, they always think they can corrupt girls, change them, push them back into the mainstream. They think girls are weak and can be easily manipulated.* I believed him. But sleeping in a bed was definitely better than sleeping on a floor.

I turned twenty in May and spent most of that summer doing my community service at the local Salvation Army store where I could zone out or make dumb conversation with the other kids working their hours while sorting through donated clothes and household goods.

I attended the drug and alcohol education classes as required, usually with the smell of booze still on my breath. I still remember what we were taught about drugs—that illegal substances could adversely affect your health—but I wasn't paying attention to the part about drinking. Alcohol was considered perfectly acceptable in white power and therefore wasn't an issue I felt I needed to address. We'd always been okay with drinking until we dropped or chain-smoking cigarettes, but if anyone touched marijuana or anything illegal, they were seen as a pariah amongst the Hammerskins. We'd boast, "We're better than the rest of society because we don't touch drugs." Drugs, we preached, were being shoved down the throats of white kids by Jews and mainstream sheep to keep them docile. In a strange way, I figured the movement's no-drug policy had helped me by preventing me from getting deeper into that scene. However, there was nothing wrong with binge drinking. Nothing at all.

Two or three nights a week I went out drinking with friends, either from the movement or Marco from high school who'd often remind me that I was unique, not the outcast I'd thought I'd been in school. We'd meet at bars where I'd down vodka, rye whiskey, Jack Daniels, Strongbow cider or Jaeger Bombs (a shot of Jaegermeister in a glass of Red Bull or some other energy drink) that got me loaded really fast. Most nights we'd drink for six or more hours, staying until closing time. Saturday nights I'd drink with Steve and the crew; we'd start around five in the afternoon and finish around midnight. On the off nights, when I was at home, I usually drank beer.

I knew I'd be going to another college in the fall to study cabinet-making so this was pretty much free time as far as I was concerned. I figured everything would work itself out, that I could continue drinking and partying and the future would take care of itself. My ambition lay in merely finishing my college course; I gave no thought to anything beyond that.

JEANETTE

When Lauren started her interior design program, I dropped her off at the bus stop every morning and picked her up well after dinner each night. Listening to her frustrations, I knew it was just a matter of time before things went south. Having her own laptop had been a college requirement so I knew nothing of her online presence or activities but, from what I could see, she spent most of the time on her computer chatting with her white power friends instead of completing assignments. I wasn't surprised when the school called to say she wasn't trying and that she was, in fact, failing. It looked to me as though she'd thrown away yet another opportunity with nary a backward glance and I made it plain she'd be paying the tuition back herself.

I had also made Lauren responsible for obtaining her own defence counsel through Legal Aid. She was legally an adult and I figured I'd suffered enough financial losses at her hands. I'd done everything I could think of for her including providing a comfortable home, lots of love and hi-speed internet. At some point, I figured it was time she learned how to help herself.

I liked her lawyer. He was great with Lauren, had a solid reputation and was willing to help but, at our first meeting, he asked why I hadn't hired him myself. It seemed the world kept expecting me to pay for my daughter's mistakes.

"You do know she stole my credit card and racked up $2800.00 in charges, right?" I asked him incredulously. "And you know that I had to put up my house as bail?" He nodded. "Am I the only one here who thinks it ironic that should I pay for her defence when I'm the victim?"

We discussed what she should and shouldn't say on the way to court that morning. I was hoping she'd listen to my suggestions, especially as most of it was what her father would have told her. "Just say, Yes, Your Honour. Even if it's not what you want to hear," I coached. "And for God's sake don't tell him you're still in white power."

But no, not Lauren. Her "I'm right, you're wrong" attitude remained firmly in place, just as it had been since joining the movement. I couldn't get her to understand her future depended on looking and sounding repentant, even if she wasn't. When she started mouthing off at the judge—"it's not about hate, it's about pride"—I felt like throwing in the towel. How could she be so stupid? So blindly stubborn and frustratingly idiotic? I hadn't asked her to put aside her ideals, even though I kept hoping she would. I'd simply asked her to behave as if she was sorry. I was relieved when the judge showed leniency. She was lucky.

Having Lauren home again was a double-edged sword. For the most part, she followed the rules and I was relieved to have her off the streets, well fed and relatively safe. At the same time, she was over eighteen and I was working all day, so I had little idea who she spent time with and what she did when away from home. I no longer stayed awake listening for the front door to open. I wasn't totally comfortable with the amount of time she spent with Marco even though he seemed pleasant, happy with her friendship and protective of her. I would have preferred she find friends who were less into partying and more interested in their future.

Neither of us brought up white power. I learned to keep my thoughts to myself and was definitely conscious of what came out of my mouth, watching her reactions to gauge how conversations affected her. There were still times when she'd fly off the handle and threaten, "I'll leave. You don't want me here anyway." Losing my temper wasn't an option if I wanted us to succeed so, instead, I practised patience, something I'd never had in spades. I'd take a deep breath before reminding her of two things. "First of all, I love you. You are my child and you are just as much a member of this family as your brother and I. Secondly, there is a jail cell waiting for you in Lindsay if you violate your court order. Do you want to screw up everything you've achieved so far?"

Thanks to Steve's steadying influence—I say that as a naive mother who was just happy he had a job and house of his own—Lauren settled down dramatically. He'd often spend the weekends with us, sleeping in the spare room at first out of respect for my son and me, joining us for dinner and discussing sports and TV shows with my son. Since Steve had his own place and Lauren spent every other weekend there, I knew they were intimate, but it took several months for me to bend, to allow them to sleep together at our house—and only after my son agreed. "No animal noises," he laughingly threatened, "or I'm outta here."

I was puzzled by Lauren and Steve's relationship. They'd spend hours up in her room, with Lauren texting friends and Steve watching movies or texting his own buddies. Sometimes they'd join my son and me, watching movies in the den, with Lauren often falling asleep on the couch before the first commercial aired. They rarely went out, were content to stay at home like an old married couple and appeared to me more like friends than lovers.

Lauren spent time with Steve's family, who welcomed her into their home and, although I don't know how Lauren spoke of me to Steve, he was nothing but respectful. Through him, I think she began to see us a little differently. Gradually her icy exterior melted, her flashing temper settling to a tiny flame that flared only occasionally. Best of all, she began to show interest in her future, opting for a nearby college that enabled her to maintain her friendships with Steve and the others while providing minimal but necessary separation from us.

CHAPTER FOURTEEN

Infiltrating the Mainstream

LAUREN

By September 2010, I was ready to give college another try. This time, I was a little smarter, choosing to study cabinetmaking and woodworking at Humber College in Toronto, something I'd always enjoyed in high school. In fact, I think it was the only class I never skipped.

I lived in residence in a tiny private room with a single bed and wooden desk, a major contrast to my room at home, which was the size of most master bedrooms. Steve lived fifteen minutes away so I could hop on the bus and see him anytime, unlike many of the girls at school who were breaking up with high school boyfriends studying at schools hundreds of miles away. Privately, I enjoyed the white power music scene but hid my beliefs and my love of aggressive music from the others in my dorm building. I didn't want to violate my probation agreement—that would have been a pain in the ass, trouble I didn't want—and the movement's paranoia said the administration would throw me out if they knew what I was into.

I was what we called "a wolf in sheep's clothing," someone who held white power beliefs but wasn't obvious, behaving in a mainstream way in public and getting a good education. Before joining the Hammerskins, my principal skills had been defending myself in a fight and knowing how to argue well for our beliefs. Now the idea was to infiltrate society, to change policies or influence others, usually by dressing in suits, working in high-powered positions and blending in with the general public. The Hammerskins talked about getting along, coexisting with people of other races so we'd come across as nonviolent, so we could turn white power from a fringe group into a mainstream movement.

Ronan, who had brought me into the Hammerskins, was getting married and I was invited to the wedding, held on the grounds of his fiancée's family mansion in Caledon. Ronan was always nice to me except when he reminded me, "You once hung out on the streets with the bad part of the movement," meaning Donny, Raymond and Bentley. His fiancée was nice too, a submissive, quiet, typical house-wife type of girl.

A group of us—Steve and I, the other guys from the band—were preaching, blowing smoke at each other and drinking till we dropped when a fight broke out between the bride's uncle and Dustin, one of our members. When the uncle said, "White people have no place being in Canada. This is the Natives' land," Dustin countered with, "The white people were actually here first. The history books were written by the Jews to make us look bad."

Things got really heated then. I was sitting next to Dustin's wife who asked, "Can one of you guys pull him away?"

The guys just laughed. "He's fine, he's just having a little conversation."

"No, one of you needs to pull him away," she insisted. It was then we heard someone crashing into a table of wine glasses, realizing too late that Dustin had knocked the uncle over. After apologizing to his wife for not helping sooner, I felt disgusted. Was that really necessary? Couldn't he even behave at a wedding?

For all their talk about blending in, these guys had no boundaries and just didn't care. Most members spent more time fighting (provok-ing people in bars so they'd be the ones to start the fight), partying and talking a good line than actively forwarding the cause by distributing flyers or organizing rallies, unless Paul Fromm was involved.

Shortly after the wedding, I received a Facebook message from Paul Fromm, who wrote he was running for mayor of Mississauga that October on a platform of anti-immigration. He'd run for various political parties and school board positions before (he wanted to influence kids to his way of thinking) but had never won. His campaign this time, when I researched it, seemed pointless because I was pretty certain immigration was a federal issue, not municipal, but I went to his meeting anyway.

Paul's meeting began with his usual, "Mass immigration and cultural Marxism are an ongoing threat to our society" speech. The media, he always complained, focused only on certain parts of his speeches. "Trying to make me out as a fool, but I can back up my points with research."

"It's a 'freeze immigration' policy," he explained this time. "My message isn't that I want to kick all the immigrants out of the country. Rather, it's that we don't need any *more* immigrants." He claimed train stations in the city looked like "flippin' Calcutta" and that the city had been "paved over with tacky houses that are mostly filled with East Indians." Mississauga was a diverse city, just as neighbouring Toronto was, so people looked at him like an undesirable when he spoke. Everyone that is, except us. His ideology made so much sense to us.

Once the speech was over, a group of us went out for coffee to discuss how we could help Paul's campaign by coming up with ways to keep the interest of his audience, who were mostly white power guys. Most of them liked the idea of having women serving drinks and food at party meetings, so that, rather than politics, became their focus. "They have to be good-looking women," they agreed. I didn't have a problem serving them. In fact, I liked the validation I got when they'd tell me I was attractive, a good woman and how lucky Steve was to have me.

At one of Fromm's rallies, I was introduced to Caleb, a Confederate Hammerskin who'd spent sixteen years in a Texas jail for the racially motivated drive-by shooting of a Black man back in 1991. He hadn't been the one to pull the trigger, but he hadn't stopped it from happening either. Canadian born, Caleb had moved to Texas as a kid; that was where he first started engaging in organized hate groups. Released and deported after serving his sentence, he'd come back to Toronto to rejoin the movement. I noticed him sitting at the front of the room; thickly built, broad-shouldered and clean-shaven, he seemed attentive yet strangely desensitized. His eyes were blank but he had a slight smirk on his face. I'd met other hardened guys in the movement but had never seen any quite as dangerous looking as him.

In the end, Paul Fromm's mayoral campaign included good-looking serving women and white supremacist and Holocaust denial literature, all peppered with racist and homophobic slurs. He finished ninth of seventeen candidates with 917 votes.

I'd been at college for a month or so and was doing well in my courses. I felt as if I belonged in residence and finally began feeling confident and comfortable in my skin, even though I was still drinking heavily. Like any college kid, I built a tower in my dorm window but, instead of the usual pizza boxes, mine was made out of empty beer bottles.

Since none of my white power friends lived in residence and I was dressing like everyone else, I was free to enjoy new friends. At the lunch table one day, two guys from my class, JD and Shemar, asked me, "Do girls like anal sex?"

I started to laugh. "If a guy knows what he's doing, then, yes. An ex of mine rammed it in once without lube and it hurt like hell, so don't do that."

Shemar was Black, a class clown with a great imagination who looked more like a rocker than a "gangsta." I felt odd speaking to him at first because I'd been told Black guys would try to rape me and were offended by colour jokes. But Shemar joked about being Black all the time and shared my dirty sense of humour. "Let's have sex week," he suggested once.

"What's that?"

"Everything we say has to be about sex."

For that entire week, our tagline was, "If it's not about your dick, I don't want to hear it." That was the thing with Shemar—as long as you were fun, you were cool. With him, I didn't need to filter myself; I could respond to his jokes without stopping to consider what came out of my mouth. I'd egg him on and he'd tell us crazy stories while doing unmentionable things to the classroom equipment. Eventually, those four or five hours I spent in class each day felt like a vacation from my outside life. In the movement, I'd often end up arguing with the guys over stupid stuff but with my classmates, I never felt like I needed to compete to be heard. I never told Steve or Jan about my friendship with Shemar, only that I'd made friends, had a good class and got along with everyone. *Good to hear,* Jan replied.

Strangely, Shemar never asked me what 1488 meant, but another classmate, Brandon, who played in an NSBM band, knew and shared my beliefs. He confided that he was secretly dating a Filipino girl, something none of his bandmates knew. Here was someone else who wasn't entirely comfortable in the movement.

Brandon and I befriended a metalhead named Jackson, a guy who reminded me of my younger self—rebellious and opposed to the mainstream for no apparent reason. The three of us were messaging each other one night, sharing stories; later I told Brandon about Aaron, my elementary school friend who'd been bullied. Offline, I began recalling some of my better childhood memories and realized how much I missed Aaron. I started wondering what he was doing and how he'd fared in life, knowing I'd befriended him for the right reasons, as opposed to what I'd been doing since joining the movement, namely recruiting new members.

I had the movement and my friends from the Hammerskins but what had I given up for them? It had taken Shemar's friendship to bring out my sense of humour—one of the sides of my personality I'd thrown away. In addition, I'd given up some of my favourite mainstream metal music, repressed my own sexuality and tossed away the possibility of a career because I was unable to hold down a job.

Although education was important to the Hammerskins, I was continually shamed for my choice of college program and career. "Construction's for men," they'd jeer. "College is great, but you should have picked a different course, one meant for women." Steve seemed intimidated by my career choice but never spoke of it and happily accepted all the furniture I built for him. The sole exception was Jan: *Make me something and ship it out.*

I began to find it increasingly difficult to reconcile the Hammerskins' misogynistic comments with my own views on women. I attended a lot of events that the wives and girlfriends didn't, so I felt as though I was a crucial part of the group, as important as the guys. They told me I did more for them than any of the other girls so, in my mind, I was just as involved as any of them. But, over time, various members told me what they expected. "Act more feminine." "Avoid getting into fistfights, that's for us guys to do." "If you think you're going to be fighting on the frontlines, you can go join up with Antifa."

I also started to notice that every conversation came back to my relationship with Steve, how my choices affected him and his future. I'd joke about being on my knees in front of him, bringing him beer on command, calling him "master" in jest. One night, Rolo—a really tall Polish guy with a huge beer gut and enough facial hair to make me think of a sasquatch—started lecturing me. "Stop living this feminist college bullshit," he advised in his deep voice. "It's not good for you or Steve. Just move in with him, get married and pop out his kids. He makes enough money to support both of you."

In my heart, I'd always known I wanted more out of life—more involvement in the movement—than just having kids. My time in the Evergreen program had confirmed that I wasn't comfortable with them and I never wanted to be like their mothers—the housewife thing just wasn't me. I also noticed how the guys with stay-at-home wives and kids would often shame them, bitching about how easy they had it, hanging around all day while their husbands worked long hours to support them. Some of the guys brought their wives to shows and parties and I'd see these women, some of whom had been strippers before getting involved with the Hammerskins, standing around looking lost and lonely. Many seemed unhappy to me but, because I usually hung out with the guys, I rarely spoke to them. I don't know if they confided in each other or just sucked it up and stuck to their roles, but they continued to show up to support their men.

I knew I wasn't parent material but, when lectured about my responsibility to continue the white race, it was easier to respond, "I will. Eventually." Meanwhile, I preached anti-feminist rhetoric, and even wrote a tune, "The Anti-feminist Song." I wanted to belong, but I knew I was a hypocrite.

On the night of October 23, Steve and I were at Braedon's house watching the UFC fight between Brock Lesnar—we cheered for him because he was white—and Cain Velasquez, who eventually won the fight amid our chants of, "Come on, get that dirty spick." When he was declared the winner, the guys were utterly disgusted but, as it was a bachelor party, they eventually turned off the TV and ordered an escort for the groom-to-be. "Just make sure you send us a white girl."

A Russian woman with bleached blond hair and heavy makeup arrived to dance for the guys. I wasn't uncomfortable with the stripper or the situation, although I did find it odd that a group that condemned pornography had ordered an escort. Some of the wives left but I stuck around, drinking shots of vodka until I blacked out.

When I awoke in my dorm the following morning, I texted Steve. *What happened?* I laughed when he told me that I'd blacked out and that the stripper had taken off my shirt and bra before grinding on top of me. I knew many of the guys would have been secretly fascinated but apparently others decided that they hadn't liked what they'd seen. The following day they apologized to Steve, "Our women shouldn't act that way. So sorry, brother."

I was speechless. "I'm a white power chick who knows the ideology," I argued when I found my voice. "I'm not like their girlfriends who are there because they like a Hammerskin guy. I'm one of them."

None of that seemed to matter. Even though they'd probably egged the stripper on, they'd apologized to Steve. They were more concerned about him, his status, than they were about me. Steve hadn't felt it necessary to defend me and that really hurt. For the first time, I clearly saw that, when push came to shove, I wasn't as appreciated by the group as I'd thought. Still, they were my friends, part of my life that I couldn't imagine being without.

JEANETTE

My father had been a carpenter in England and during his first years in Canada. Paul had also enjoyed woodworking, teaching both kids how to saw, nail and sand wood. Lauren always enjoyed painting, arts and crafts, building with Lego blocks and woodworking had been her favourite elective. So it was no surprise to see Lauren wanted to take up that trade. I was optimistic it would be a good fit.

When Lauren left for college that fall, I also had high hopes she'd leave the movement behind. She seemed happier at college than she had in high school and told me she'd made friends with some of her classmates, despite differences in colour, religion and beliefs. She'd talk about Shemar, how cool and funny he was, and how great some of the other guys were.

We spoke at least once a week. I usually initiated the calls but she didn't seem to mind talking with me even when she was on her way out. I was pleased she was pulling down good marks, attending classes and making friends. All I'd ever wanted was for her to feel comfortable and accepted for herself so hearing that she was trading dirty jokes with a classmate was music to my ears. It had been a long time since I'd heard her laugh, since she'd behaved like a normal kid. She rarely mentioned the parties she attended with Steve and the Hammerskins. That was okay—I'd asked her not to discuss white power.

I thought Lauren was beginning to see how important education was to her future, how that future depended on her learning to fit into the workplace no matter the circumstances or ethnic diversity. After the fiasco of the interior design course, I'd made it clear that, if she failed this time, she'd be paying off the entire student loan I'd pressed her to apply for, rather than just a token sum.

One of Lauren's first projects was a spice rack, which she gifted to me, tangible proof that we were getting along better. What I also received were repeated requests for more money. Her dorm, food and supplies were paid for by the fund her dad and I had set up when she was born; combined with a reasonable allowance from her dad's estate, she should have had no trouble making ends meet. Instead, she was always broke, her cellphone bill well over the marginal limit I'd set. I didn't question where the money was going in case I lost her for good and convinced myself it was more important to fork over the cash than to argue. But I was getting tired of being her personal bank machine.

CHAPTER FIFTEEN

A Man's World

LAUREN _____

In the spring of 2011, the Southern Ontario Skinheads (SOS), an independent group of fifteen or so guys (and their hangers-on girl-friends) who'd befriended the Hammerskins in the hopes of an alliance, organized a concert at Legion Hall in London, Ontario. Steve's band would be playing for a crowd of approximately sixty people.

At the concert I met Max, the leader of SOS, a jerk who was a friend of Brianna's and who liked to start fights. When he realized who I was, he began making fun of me, bringing up the story of my beating two years before, until he finally asked, "Why didn't you defend yourself?"

"Pretty hard to do when it's four against one," I responded. I wanted to tell him to fuck off but, being a female, I knew I was less important than he was. If we started arguing, the guys would prob-ably take his side. By the end of the concert I'd decided if Max was going to be hanging around the Hammerskins, I'd be there less, or at least hanging out at the opposite end of the room.

A guy named Kevin, new to the Hammerskins, also showed up. Because he asked too many questions—not the kind someone would normally ask—we were immediately suspicious of him. Some of the guys suspected he was wearing a wire. When I asked if I could friend him on Facebook, he told me, "I don't use that," something else that seemed strange.

Out of curiosity, I looked Kevin up on Facebook the next day. His profile displayed some interesting pictures—in some he was with girls of colour or holding a Russian flag—that made me think he might be an Antifa member trying to infiltrate our group. I stayed quiet, not wanting to make trouble by ratting him out because he was also going to Humber College. The last thing I needed was for him to see me with Shemar and blab about my friendship with a Black guy.

A new crew was hatched in Toronto that summer. Referred to as C38 (Crew 38, the "38" standing for crossed hammers, the Hammerskins logo), they were a "support" and probationary crew for the Hammerskins. They held monthly meetings and once someone had proven themselves by starting a bar fight or something similar, they'd get a Hammerskin patch, if the crew approved. Steve seemed to enjoy being involved in this new club, which I found odd. Apart from playing drums for the band, he'd always been more of a "hang around" guy, someone on the fringes of the Hammerskins who enjoyed socializing more than spreading the word. He had never had a Hammerskin patch but the guys seemed to accept him, although they would question his commitment whenever I'd shown up at parties without him. Now, all of a sudden, here he was sporting a patch. I don't know what he had to do to get it and couldn't bring myself to congratulate him, especially since he seemed to be more in my face about having kids than ever before.

Alliances and infighting were common among groups within the movement. The Hammerskins had a serious beef with American Volksfront (People's Front), an "international fraternal organization for persons of European descent." Founded in the US in 1994, the group claimed to be nonviolent, even though they were linked to various racially motivated attacks. They had about fifty members in the US and another fifty in Europe and elsewhere.

I'd met one of their members, Carey, online, through Stormfront's white power forum and was comfortable talking to him, more about our personal lives rather than the movement itself, mainly because he didn't seem interested in the idea of women in submissive roles. We'd remained friends throughout the year he spent in a US prison for parole violation, mostly through written letters. I knew I was expected to cut contact with him because Steve was a patched member of C38, but I refused, reasoning that I was not a patched member so I could speak to anyone I wanted. He was due to be released from jail and the guys from C38, who'd seen him on my Facebook friends list, bugged me to be their pawn, to set him up for a fall because he was in a rival group. "Pretend you're single," they urged, "Send him nude pictures and get him to come up to Canada so we can beat him up."

"No," I told them over and over again.

"But you're the girlfriend of a C38 guy," they protested. "You should be on our side."

I flatly refused. No way was I going to do that to a friend, someone who I'd begun to realize treated me far better than the guys I was currently hanging out with. Carey listened to me while these guys from C38 were beginning to sound like pompous morons.

Kevin, the guy suspected of spying, received a patch but the C38 guys became even more suspicious when he didn't show up regularly at meetings. Another member found the same Facebook pictures and information I had, which made them all the more certain he'd been trying to infiltrate the group. When his absences continued, a few of the C38 guys decided to break into his house and steal some of his things, including his patch, effectively kicking him out.

I don't know if Kevin was a spy or if he just wanted to leave but, either way, I think he was afraid of the repercussions. Leaving was not an easy option. If you considered it, you'd be either "convinced" to stay or beaten up. The C38 members would dish out whatever punishment they thought appropriate to anyone exiting, just like the other white power groups I'd known. Although I wasn't patched (women weren't important enough to be patched), I knew I wouldn't be exempt.

I graduated from Humber College in September 2011 and a week later Carey was released from prison. I messaged him immediately, happy to hear he was alive and reasonably well, all things considered. I had no idea what had gone through his head during his year in prison, what troubles he'd survived, and I didn't want to imagine them either. We spoke on the phone regularly as he put his life back together but, as the weeks passed, I sensed a change in him. He wasn't inclined to talk about the movement, a certain disconnect in his tone suggesting a lack of commitment. Months after his release from jail, he told me he was no longer with Volksfront. "There was a lot of drama in our circles so I've decided to leave."

He'd been seriously committed to the movement once upon a time; his exit showed me that even the most committed could crack. I respected his need to start fresh and hoped he would stay in touch with me but I also realized that, as sick as I was of hearing about the whole thing, I wasn't yet ready to leave myself. The risks were too high and, if I left the movement, I'd lose the tightknit group I enjoyed being part of.

That fall, the Hammerskins hosted another concert at a Legion Hall in Barrie, about an hour north of Toronto, hoping that the hall's location in the middle of nowhere would discourage a police presence. Most of the Hammerskins showed up, along with the Southern Ontario Skinheads and some independent white nationalists. In addition to local bands, several others played, including the Vinland Warriors from Quebec and a girl named Sara from Ottawa, who wrote her own acoustic white power music.

Sara was first on stage. I was amazed by her singing voice and skilled guitar playing. Looking around, I noticed most of the guys were talking right through her entire set. At one point, when introducing a song she'd written in memory of fallen skinheads from the early days, she asked for a moment of silence from the audience. When nobody quieted down, she got frustrated, finally yelling out, "I hate to be a bitch on stage but could I have everyone please shut the fuck up?"

That's when I realized how little the mostly male audience valued her performance. It shocked me to see how under-appreciated she was as a female musician and triggered memories of when Poppa had asked me to play the clarinet at family gatherings.

"Let's hear you play something," he'd say once dinner was finished and we'd all be sitting together in the living room.

After some coaxing, I'd pull out my clarinet and one of the pieces I'd been practising and begin playing. Less than a minute later he'd start talking right over it, as if it were background music, as if I weren't even there.

As a child I hadn't been able to ask why. And now, as a female in the movement I still felt unable to speak up for myself. I began to see other similarities between my past and the treatment I'd been receiving from the guys in the movement. In school I'd been put down because of my weight and clothing choices; now the Hammerskins were forcing similar gender roles on me. The pressure to have children was coming at me constantly from Steve, the crew and even my mother, who wanted grandkids. I'd felt disconnected from what I'd considered femininity; now my role was to be one of subservience, to give birth to and raise the kids who would "continue the white race." I'd see Hammerskins parents dressing their kids in fatigues and remember my parents enforcing their "no piercings, no dying your hair, no tattoos" rules.

I still wasn't quite ready to dig further into these issues, so I made for the mosh pit that started up after Sara's set when the local bands began to play. It was a relief to bump and knock around with others at the foot of the stage. I jumped in along with Mandy, a tough, thickly built girl the guys made fun of, often referring to her as a Femi-Nazi. I really liked her and we'd high-five each other every time we struggled out of the pit. She eventually pulled me aside and asked,

"Hey, so aside from you and me, are there any real skinbyrds here? Or just wives?"

"Most of them are the guys' wives. Why are you asking?"

"Cause we're the only ones who seem remotely interested in any of this," she replied. When I looked around, I saw she was right; we were the only females in a mosh pit filled with white power guys. Every other woman was clustered in a tightknit group far away from the action.

In spite of all the booze I drank that night, I could still scream, "I hate commie scum!" while up on stage with the Vinland Warriors. I'd always been able to death growl and had been praised for my singing but I think it freaked out some of the guys to hear a slight blond chick giving it up with the band. I made sure to enjoy it because at night's end I knew I'd get the usual reminder, "It's your ultimate duty to give Steve as many kids as he wants."

Weeks later, I found out Steve and his C38 buddies were preparing a targeted attack against a group of Black guys. Thinking about how he might get hurt, I asked him, "If you had kids, how would you explain the bruises from your fights to them?"

"White kids aren't going to be safe if we allow these Blacks to walk all over us. We're defending our people." His answer was the one I'd heard many times before but this time it got me thinking about parenting a child of hate. If a child saw evidence of their parent's fight, what impact would that have? Was it fair to raise a child in this culture? What about parents who forced their opinions on their kids?

Traumatic memories had begun surfacing from my own violent past, like the beating my "friends" had given me and the mental health issues that distressed me. Tired of defending my choices, desperate to feel healthy in my mind, I finally set clear boundaries with Steve in front of our friends. "This isn't an appropriate time for me to think about having kids," I said. "I'm twenty-one and right now I'm dealing with past traumas."

Of course, the responses from the group were rude and ignorant.

"That's no excuse not to have kids" and "Just get over it and don't drop the baby," they laughed. If this group claimed to be defending and fostering the future of white people, shouldn't they care about the health of the mothers of their children? If their talk was all about protecting and caring for their women, why throw aside my issues as if they were unimportant?

I still cared about Steve and didn't want to break up with him because then I'd be alone. And there seemed to be nothing else waiting for me that was worth leaving the movement for. Still, I was finally starting to think for myself.

After graduation, I immediately started looking for work as a cabinet-maker somewhere reasonably close to Steve and the crew. One of the callbacks I received was from a Polish-sounding guy who ran a small millwork shop in Mississauga. The Toronto white power movement was bursting with eastern Europeans who'd taught me to swear in Polish and since my impression of skilled trades was that workers didn't need to keep their language clean, I figured this was a good omen. Around this time, I decided to stop wearing makeup and traded my knee-high boots for steel-toed work boots, regulation in most millwork shops.

Mississauga was too far from Whitby for an easy commute so I also answered an ad for a cheap place to rent, a room in a condo owned by a lady with two cats, and took my written driver's test, knowing I'd eventually need to learn to drive. Three things accomplished in one week, I congratulated myself. Things were going well despite the many warnings I'd received that I couldn't be a white power advocate and still lead a good life. So much for their predictions. Those who'd warned me, those outside of the movement, really needed to stop listening to what the Jewish media told them.

At the job interview, Aleksy, the Polish man with whom I'd spoken earlier, shook my hand and asked, "How old are you?"

"I'm twenty-one."

"Oh boy, you're young, eh?" he said as we sat down in his office.

His next comment threw me off. "So, I have no idea why in hell you want this job."

"I've always enjoyed practical work," I told him, "as opposed to learning from books."

"Okay, what does your family think of you doing this?"

I wanted to tell him that not long before I'd been living on the streets, that my family would have given anything just to hear that I had a decent job. Instead, I said, "My mom and brother are supportive of it."

"And your father?" Aleksy pressed. "What does he think? Surely, he would be concerned about you working with men all day, wouldn't he?"

"My dad passed away five years ago so I can't assume anything," I answered.

"I'm sorry to hear that," he said. He showed me the workshop, which was a huge mess. I guessed what my responsibilities as a new employee would be: cleaning the place.

He ended the interview and surprised me by saying, "Let's give it a try and see how you do. You can start next week." Shaking hands, I thanked him for his time, but on my bus ride to view the condo, I wondered why he'd asked such personal questions. Nonetheless, I was happy to be given the chance and looked forward to the following week.

After handing over first and last month's rent for my room—provided by my mom as I had nothing but a huge student debt—I walked to the bus stop pretty happy with myself, excited to tell Steve, who lived twenty minutes away from the condo, about my job and my new place. When I got to his place that afternoon he didn't say much. I eventually broke the silence with a joke. "So, should I go make your sandwich now? I'll be one of those feminists during the workday and your little slave in the evenings."

Steve replied, "I got no problem with that."

As much as I thought what we shared was love, I had to admit he wasn't as supportive as I would have liked, and I was glad I wasn't moving in with him. I wanted to live my own life first, and maybe I was afraid to see how we'd been slowly drifting apart.

"I'm going to save for a truck," I told him.

His only response was, "Make sure it's got a crew cab for when we have kids."

Ten minutes early on my first day at work, I stood outside smoking a cigarette, waiting for Aleksy to arrive. When he pulled up, I greeted him. "Morning. How are you?"

"What's that?" he asked, pointing to my smoke.

"Yeah, I smoke. I have for a few years," I replied with a laugh.

"You should quit," he said. "It doesn't look nice when girls smoke."

How often was I going to be reminded of my gender? I wondered.

Soon after starting work, my back began bothering me and I mentioned to Steve that I was thinking of getting a massage.

"Great idea," he said. "You'll need a strong back to carry our children." Fuck, it's still coming from all directions, I thought.

With the exception of me and a Hispanic guy named Roberto who was working for Aleksy while his own workplace was temporarily shut down, every one of the seven or eight men in the workshop was Polish. They were all in their fifties and sixties, clean-cut, of average build and all except the two finishers were cabinetmakers. Roberto seemed to be the only one who wasn't old-fashioned. One day when I dropped the F-bomb, one of the men reminded me of Poppa when he said, "That doesn't sound nice coming from a lady."

The Polish guys made no effort to include me—or Roberto, who also didn't speak their language—in conversations. I'd spend breaks in the corner, not understanding what they said, or speaking with Roberto who let me help him with his work, rather than expecting me to clean up after him. I thought I'd been hired to sand and finish the cabinets, not just to clean the workshop but Roberto was the only one who allowed me to build or sand anything. When he left at the end of his two-week stint, I missed him and felt more alone than ever. Sure, he was Hispanic, but he'd included me, willingly teaching me what the others wouldn't.

Jarek, one of the Poles, soon began lecturing me on why I shouldn't listen to heavy metal music, alleging young kids committed mass murders and shooting sprees as a result of it. When that didn't work, he talked about God and tried to convert me to his religion. I tried to be respectful, telling him Christianity didn't resonate with me, but he kept saying, "Eventually you'll come to see the light." It frustrated me to have people continually challenging my lifestyle and choices, but I stayed quiet because I really needed the job.

Three weeks after I'd started work, Aleksy called me into his office. "I'm letting you go. The other guys don't like working with a girl."

Apparently, even though the shop was clean and I'd done what was asked, they'd told him I was unable to do certain tasks, even though I could, and that I didn't fit in, which finally made sense to me. No wonder they'd never spoken English—they'd been talking about me. I knew Jarek was pissed at my defence of metal music and unwilling-ness to discuss religion at work and so I'd been excluded.

I couldn't complain about sexism because I'd preached anti-feminist rhetoric myself, often advocating for women to be in roles of subservience. What ran through my head as I walked back to the condo was, I guess I don't belong in the trades. What had I been thinking, taking that college course? I felt dejected, fed up. All I had was a student debt and nothing to show for it.

Stopping at the liquor store, I grabbed some booze, went up to my room and did what I normally did—drank myself to sleep. When my mom called to offer encouragement, "Keep looking, keep trying. Something's out there for you," all I could think was, it's just not worth it.

Shortly after losing my job at Aleksy's, my landlady, whom I'd nicknamed Baba Yaga (witch-woman in Polish) evicted me for no reason. With my mom's help, I moved back to Whitby and started looking for work, even though I didn't think carpentry was for me.

One day my mom and I ran into a woman at Home Depot who knew an independent contractor in Oshawa in need of a helper. Within my first week of working for Staszek, we were getting along famously—even drinking together during lunch breaks, when a bottle of vodka and a chaser would appear on the table. He seemed like the kind of boss anyone would want to work for. He was lax, lenient about time and a smoker himself, so he didn't mind me having a lit cigarette while I was working.

We were both drunk one day when, fed up with him bugging me about my 1488 tattoo, I burst out, "I'm white power. I believe that defending my people is a social duty, not an antisocial crime."

Staszek started laughing and said, "I'm white, just like you, so I'm not going to say anything against it." I felt relieved since it didn't seem he'd fire me for my beliefs. In fact, I even tossed around the idea of inviting him to our next show because he'd once told me, "Pakis have dots on their foreheads so you've got a target to aim for when you shoot them." Like many of his generation, Staszek used the term Paki to describe anyone from the Indian subcontinent, not realizing that Pakistan is largely Muslim and it's Hindus, mostly from India, who have red tikkas.

Overall, I enjoyed the work, using my hands to help create doors and kitchen units, custom cabinetry and furniture. When Staszek's touchy-feely ways escalated into sexual harassment, I stayed quiet. I was slowly building a career and wanted to keep my job.

JEANETTE

My son, my mom and I were so proud of Lauren for sticking with her course and graduating with her diploma, ready for a future career she could enjoy. I was equally pleased and proud when she found work right away but wasn't surprised by the old-fashioned attitudes she encountered at both Aleksy's and Staszek's workshops. Having graduated from a male-dominated program and having worked in the fields of land surveying and civil engineering for many years myself, I knew how prevalent stereotypes and biases were against women in trades. Lauren was quick to grow frustrated and angry, ready to throw aside what she'd accomplished simply because others had put her off, so I fought an uphill battle to convince her she needed to be stronger, quicker, more eager and willing than everyone else if she was to succeed in a man's world. I hated having to explain to her that a woman working in trades had to keep her distance from male coworkers, that the minute she let down her guard she'd be branded as easy and willing.

I knew that both Lauren and Steve were still involved with white power but chose not to examine their involvement too closely. As I hadn't allowed Lauren to discuss the movement at home, I really knew nothing about it and still considered Steve a calming, steady influence. As far as I could see, she and Steve were fringe members who needed to break away from the rest in order to have a decent, caring relationship. I was concerned that Lauren would break up with him and find herself adrift again. Still, even though I made no secret of my desire for grandchildren, I knew better than to push a future that might include a family.

The day Lauren was to move out of the condo, I showed up with a moving van, ready to take her home. There was never a question of her moving in with Steve. He didn't seem ready to commit, to have her share his house or his life outside of the movement or their parties, and I don't think Lauren wanted that kind of commitment either. She seemed wounded, beaten down by losing both her new job and her residence. It was as if she needed to return to a place where she knew she could lick her wounds until she could get back on her feet. And I was more than ready to have her back home.

Expecting her landlady to be there with our last month's rent cheque, I was surprised when Lauren said she'd gone out shortly before I showed up. I shouldn't have been—she'd already scammed Lauren out of an extra month's rent before giving her notice to leave without cause. I asked Lauren if she'd done something to piss her off and she explained, "I asked to use the washer but she said it was broken. Then I put my food in the fridge and the next day, it was gone. She won't let me use the internet or TV." In fact, she'd promised Lauren the use of appliances that didn't work, non-existent storage space and a door that didn't lock; her cats had the run of the place, including Lauren's room, and she regularly ate food Lauren had taken to hiding in her room.

Steve had a prior commitment so the two of us lugged stuff downstairs, packed up the van, cleaned her room, patched the walls and sat down to wait. When a further hour passed, I wrote a note and taped it to the TV, asking her to mail the money as soon as possible. Moments later, as we rode the elevator to the ground floor, we struck up a conversation with a resident who told us, "Oh yeah, she does this all the time. Takes in young girls then tosses them out after a month, keeping their money. We're all fed up with her, but management won't do anything about it."

We tried for a month to make contact with the ex-landlady. When Lauren found the same ad posted on Kijiji, I decided to sue her through Small Claims Court. It took us months of frustration and time—not something I had a lot of since I'd begun a new job an hour's drive away—but eventually we won and got our money back. A difficult lesson but one neither of us will ever forget.

I didn't like Staszek the one time I met him, but it was Lauren's choice to stay or go. She worked to rein in her temper when confronted with his sexual advances, something which might once have been impossible. "Doesn't matter if you're smarter or better," I told her when she vented, yet again, about Staszek's treatment of her. Providing a few examples of my own—having been treated badly by several male coworkers and bosses over the span of twenty years—I explained, "If you party with them, some—not all—will think it's an open invitation."

Unfair as it was, Lauren's need for a paycheque and her desire to prove herself were forcing her to deal with uncomfortable situations in a mature manner, whether in her personal or professional life. For the first time, practical considerations generally overrode her anger. She was growing up.

CHAPTER SIXTEEN

Tragedy and Clarity

LAUREN

Jan and I had been emailing each other weekly for almost three years. He was non-judgmental, someone I could be honest with, say anything to. While he never told me directly how disillusioned he was, I think we were both in the same place—tired of the whole white power thing but not ready to walk away. In late fall 2011, he wrote: *What kind of brotherhood is this? Nobody's got anyone else's back.* That was a common thread I'd heard from a lot of the guys, one Jan and I had been discussing a lot lately. I responded: *Yeah, they always talk about how we need it more but I never see them doing anything about it.*

One Saturday morning in March 2012, Steve picked me up at the train near his place so I could get another tattoo from our friend Herbert. "By the way, you know that guy Jan, from out west?"

"Yeah?" I said, hoping Jan was returning to Ontario, that I might see him again.

"He died."

It was as if time stood still, as it had when I'd lost my dad, when I'd learned of Tim's overdose. I had a hard time processing Steve's words. "Yeah, he was doing collections and went to some guy's house. The homeowner says he stabbed him out of self-defence. The police found his body inside and said it appeared to be a home invasion."

Shivers ran up my spine. This couldn't be true. It had to be a rumour. A bad dream.

"The police don't know the exact details yet, but should they come asking us anything, we're going to say that we know nothing. Either that or that we heard Jan got into a drunken brawl."

I stayed silent, knowing Steve was just repeating what the Hammerskins had told him to say. He didn't care one way or the other about Jan, either as a human being or a white power member. How much of a brotherhood was this when members didn't care for one another? My image of brotherhood was different from the reality of a group where everyone covered their asses and any connection to the victim by saying, "I don't know" or giving fake stories to the police.

That weekend, while Herbert cooked Ukrainian cabbage rolls for dinner and the loud beat of RAC (Rock Against Communism) played in the background—the lyrics, as always, speaking of white brotherhood—I couldn't get Jan's death out of my mind. When Herbert asked if I wanted to start my new tattoo, I just couldn't get interested. When I got home that Sunday night, I immediately googled Jan's name and found exactly what I hadn't wanted to believe.

Jan had been stabbed to death on March 17, 2012. Two days later, the CBC website reported the following:

Police have released the name of a man killed in a stabbing in Surrey, B.C., Saturday night.

Police say Surrey resident Jan (January) Aron Korinth, 26, was pronounced dead at the scene.

Police were called to a home at about 11 p.m. PT to reports of a stabbing. A 36-year-old man was found suffering from head wounds. He was taken to hospital for treatment and later released.

A trail of blood led officers to an unresponsive man nearby who was pronounced dead at the scene.

Police say a motive has not been determined but the incident appears to be gang-related and may be a case of an attempted home invasion or break-in.

Jan had been stabbed to death. The many articles I read were consistent with one another, but when a friend of his from the movement sent an anonymous email to the media, stating that Jan was murdered because of his association with white power, I had to pause.

They . . .planned the attack, no doubt because Jan was a member of Blood and Honour. It was a hate crime against our people. We will not stop until there is justice for our fallen comrade.

The police were concerned about this veiled threat, according to the news, worried it might spark a gang war. Inflammatory comments were posted on social media while white power sites referred to Jan as a "martyr" and urged members to retaliate in what they called a race war.

I wasn't aware of any incidents where comrades were targeted by the general public. More often than not we were the ones who started the fights. Jan himself had been on probation for assault causing bodily harm, along with two WEB (Western European Bloodline) associates from Alberta who had been convicted of beating a bystander to death in 2010.

I'd got into the habit of checking the Anti-Racist Canada blog to ensure my name was no longer being published on their site. Since my probation, I had been flying under the radar, sharing as little information as possible on my Facebook and online accounts. The guys had urged me not to post anything on social media, thinking it would bring heat onto the crew.

A week after Jan's death I looked to see if they'd posted anything about him and found links to more articles. The *Huffington Post* stated there was no evidence to suggest Jan was targeted. Instead, they claimed he was the instigator, that he'd gotten involved with other criminal organizations and had died because of it. This wasn't the first time I'd heard of someone becoming involved in criminal activity outside of the movement. I knew of some members who'd dealt drugs under the radar and Donny, who used to say "no exceptions, we don't contradict ourselves," had been into credit card fraud with a bunch of Koreans.

Why did it have to be Jan? I kept asking myself as waves of hurt swamped me. I wanted a miracle—to wake up from the bad dream of his death. I couldn't focus at work and drank even more as I tried to avoid the ugly and sobering truth I didn't yet have the courage to admit—that the movement I'd been part of for five years was full of delusion.

I became more argumentative with Staszek, telling him to fuck off whenever he pissed me off; I took more smoke breaks than usual and was drinking whenever I could, my concentration at an all-time low. When Staszek finally asked why I hadn't been myself lately, I told him about Jan's death.

"Yeah? So? People die every day. Bad shit happens, but life goes on."

He didn't seem to care that I'd lost someone special. His offhand remarks stung, adding to the pain I was already feeling. No one seemed to give a shit, so eventually I told my mom. Even though she didn't know the right words, I could tell she cared. She disagreed with our beliefs but still recognized that Jan had been a good friend.

Once again, I searched the Anti-Racist Canada blog. This time I found a post entitled "Wanting or thinking of leaving the movement? Read this, please." It was a note Jan's mother had posted.

Jan was another angry young man that as a teenager on an unfortunate trip to Germany was recruited into whatever skinhead group happened to be near his father's house. He had gone to connect with his birthfather and as that had gone very badly he was easy prey for a group looking for angry, blond and blue-eyed members. Jan fit that bill perfectly at the time and that was the first time I lost my son. Now I have lost him forever. There is no connection to Blood & Honour with Jan's death and he has no real friends there. Friends don't send anonymous emails that cause incredible pain to a friend's family, spreading ludicrous stories of targeting and hate crimes. Friends don't try to swoop in and cover their own tracks and connections after "a comrade falls," friends care and help out. Turns out Jan did not have any friends like that in the city. He was, however, connected to that group, but more of a closet racist, one that didn't live his "convictions" out-loud and proud 24/7, but rather hidden away for the most part. The recruitment and brainwashing still happen all over the world like it does with any other cult and the recruits are still all looking for whatever it is in the individual cases. Other angry, young men will replace my son and other mothers will be heartbroken. Jan was also an adored big brother, a loved and loving son, grandson, cousin, nephew and friend to those of us that actually knew him.

I didn't want to show my mom the note. Not because I worried about criticism or "I told you so." Because I realized that she'd feared writing the same thing many times in the past. No parent should ever outlive their kid, I thought as I stared at the computer screen, especially under these circumstances. I understood, even through my extremist and often drunken lens, how much it had taken for Jan's mother to write the article, how painful and difficult it must have been. Sitting there, something triggered in my memory, an email my mom had written back when I was on the streets and out of contact with my family: *I know the daughter I love is still there somewhere.* I could imagine my mom writing something similar to what Jan's mother had written and it sent me reeling, yet another shock to my battered system.

What hit me hardest was Jan's mother's grief-stricken comment: *That was the first time I lost my son. Now I have lost him forever.* I remembered all the phone calls my mom had received about me from the cops. How had she felt? How had my choices affected her, my brother, our family? I knew they'd never agreed with or understood my involvement in the movement but since I'd never felt I belonged within the family it had been easy to ignore their feelings. Now that I was on good terms with my mom and brother, Jan's murder had me rethinking everything.

Jan's death, although raw and sad, finally helped bring me some much-needed clarity. There was no respect from the guys in the movement for their dead friend, someone too young to have his life cut short by stupid violence. Re-reading his mother's message, I began questioning the victim mentality I'd been seeing, hearing and living for five years. If we were the ones creating this misery for ourselves, what was the point? It was not the fault of other races or religions. We all chose to be here. And we could choose to leave.

I realized I couldn't play the victim any longer. I was tired of being angry all the time, being someone I wasn't and, most of all, I was sick of discriminating against other cultures, religions and races. After five years of being a female in a white power subculture, I was finally allowing myself to acknowledge its hypocrisy. I'd been nagged, constantly, to do my duty and have kids, to be subservient. I'd been laughed at by the Hammerskins for wanting a job in construction, told my choice of careers wouldn't suit "our ideals," belittled and used on many occasions—things my father, if he were able, would have given me hell for putting up with. I'd been discriminated against by those who expected me to discriminate against others. I had finally reached the point where I just didn't want to pretend to be someone I wasn't.

JEANETTE

My heart broke for both Jan and his mother. Any parent who has lost a child—no matter that they were part of extremism—deserves sympathy rather than scorn. I had wondered many times how it would feel to receive a call from the police saying my daughter was dead, that Lauren had been the victim of a random attack while living on the streets or, Heaven forbid, at the hands of the white supremacists she called "family." A call too late to change things, to save her life, to re-establish our relationship. Thank goodness we were spared that pain. One constant ache I carried around was the guilt of having thrown her out of the house and into their willing hands. By arguing against the movement, I'd played right into their hand, had reinforced, albeit unknowingly, every stereotype they'd fed her about parents and society.

Lauren's pain upon learning of Jan's death was very real. Although she'd rarely been in touch with her emotions and was generally slow to empathize with others, I knew she was hurting. It was evident from her demeanour, the pain on her face and in her voice that Jan had been more than just a friend to her. In person and through social media, they'd created a connection that transcended the distance between Ontario and BC. Losing Jan, losing Tim—after having lost her father—left a huge, gaping hole inside her. I was touched that she had confided me and frustrated that there seemed absolutely nothing I could do for her, aside from saying, "I'm so sorry."

Jan, in death, helped Lauren to clarify her perceptions of the movement and gave her the chance to question belief systems she'd already outgrown. Because we rarely spoke of the movement at home, I had no idea how much she was struggling but I had already begun to see tiny cracks in her tough-girl facade, small, almost imperceptible changes that gave me hope. She began participating in dinner conversations, her voice spirited, her tone respectful, even when debating politics or religion. She showed more interest in everyday happenings, in her brother's life and mine, and seemed to appreciate her Nana's love all the more.

If not for Jan's death, it would have taken Lauren a lot longer to confront the inconsistencies she'd been silently questioning for so long. That the loss of Jan's extraordinary friendship and the stark reality of his life—and death—meant nothing to the movement was the final push she needed to leave. And for that, I am grateful.

CHAPTER SEVENTEEN

Cutting Ties

LAUREN_____

In the summer of 2012, a few months after Jan's death, I went to my final white power show, hosted in the same Barrie location as the previous concert. I didn't tell anyone, not even Steve, that I'd decided to leave white power. After the beating Raymond's crew gave me and having witnessed how Kevin was treated (although I didn't know if the guys ever did beat him) I'd decided I'd have to leave gradually. It didn't matter whether you were male or female—leaving white power was not easy.

When a local band went on stage, their singer announced, "This is dedicated to our fallen brother, Jan." I felt as if I'd been punched in the gut. This movement had done nothing to acknowledge Jan's death, I thought incredulously, and yet here they are suddenly dedicating an entire set to him? They were using his death to promote their cause, something I found disgusting.

The whole situation hit me hard. I realized that, if I died tomorrow, no one would really care and they'd easily find another girl to replace me. I'd gotten involved in the movement because it had made me feel important; I'd thought I *was* important to the members. Now, I was starting to see things differently. I wanted to go home right then but couldn't because Steve had driven and I was loaded. So, I went into the mosh pit for every song, moving, smashing, pushing and bouncing around with everyone else. Only there could I release my growing anger.

Later in the evening, I climbed onstage to death growl alongside the vocalist from the band that was playing but, half-way through singing "I hate commie scum," I froze. Suddenly my conviction to the music was gone, the lyrics no longer resonating. For a second or two I stood staring at the floor of the stage, my mind totally blank. Then I jumped off the stage. As I walked through the crowd, another member called out, "You let us down, Lauren."

I didn't care anymore. Waiting for the end of the concert, I jumped back into the mosh pit, playing along. When another woman started grinding against me for fun, I thought, Why the hell not? I've done more than this with other girls, stuff I'd kept secret from Steve and the guys in the movement.

Rolo approached the two of us. "That's faggotry," he snarled. "Lesbians are contributing to the destruction of our cause."

I stopped moving. I couldn't believe he'd said that when, not even ten minutes before, I'd seen two guys jokingly grabbing each other's dicks outside the venue. Nobody had said anything to them, I thought angrily, turning my back on him. Why was it okay for them and not us? My ex-girlfriend Katy came to mind and, thinking about our short relationship, I suddenly knew it had been better than anything I'd experienced within the movement. Homosexuality and homoerotica were "unnatural" to the white power guys but, especially at that moment, they sure as hell didn't feel that way to me.

Thoughts bounced through my mind while I bumped around the mosh pit. One in particular hit me. Hate, I suddenly understood, was unnatural. Constantly having to work out every situation to ensure it fit the movement's narratives was exhausting. Seeing the world through the lens of hate hadn't kept me safe, hadn't kept me from being hurt. It had actually restricted me. It was another "a-ha" moment.

Later that night, I found myself throwing up at Steve's, something that had been happening more frequently after drinking in recent months. I was getting sick every single time I drank, waking up fatigued the following day—weak, as if I hadn't eaten in months—and generally feeling like utter crap. What was going on with me?

The morning after the show, Steve suggested, "Maybe stop drinking for a week or two and see what happens."

I agreed, even though I was a bit nervous. It had been six years since I'd been totally sober. "I'll give it a try."

"Just remember," Steve continued, "when you get pregnant you won't be able to drink at all. Better get used to it now."

That really pissed me off. Was that all he really cared about? Me having his babies, continuing the white race? Why didn't I matter as much as his future kids? "I don't ever want kids," I threw back at him. As usual he pulled the silent treatment, grumpy because he wasn't getting his way. I was sick and tired of hearing the same old crap so, twenty minutes later, I left for home.

I'd been drinking heavily almost every day since high school: after work, at home, at Steve's, at parties. I felt I needed alcohol, but more than that, I enjoyed it too. The feeling of freedom it brought, the escape it offered that had become my lifeline. It had never occurred to me to quit but I soon found out how hard it was to stop. Everything pissed me off. I felt irritable and every part of my body ached, like I had one giant case of the flu. And, after a week with no alcohol, I still felt terrible.

I went to a doctor who, after hearing my symptoms, suggested running some tests. At my follow-up appointment he told me, "You have cirrhosis of the liver. You still have enough healthy liver that you shouldn't need a transplant but let's not make it worse. You need to stop drinking immediately."

I was stunned. Drinking was a crutch I depended on. What was I going to do with myself now? Alcohol was my liquid courage, a means of finding some part of myself I could like. Who would I be sober?

I didn't have the first clue what cirrhosis of the liver was but I knew it had to be serious for him to recommend I make immediate changes. I was scared to google it, to find out exactly what it meant and I kept the diagnosis from my mom, worried I'd get lectured about it and hear, "I told you so." I thought she'd tell me it was my fault, that I should have listened to her. That was the last thing I wanted to hear.

But at least my sobriety provided me with an excuse not to attend Hammerskin functions. I'd say, "I want to stay sober. Being around people who are loaded isn't helping me" and for the most part, Steve went along with it—until he dislocated his right knee. Stuck wearing a brace for a few weeks, he couldn't drive himself.

"I'll drop you off but I'm not staying," I'd tell him.

"Doesn't it make more sense for you to come in and stay, rather than just dropping me off and picking me up later?" Frustrated at not being heard, I'd go along with him rather than argue.

I was constantly asked why I wasn't drinking. When I recounted my health scare, most of the members shrugged it off. "That's just one doctor's opinion," one guy said. "Why would you listen to him?" Another member kept pressuring me to drink. I lost count of the times I said no. All I wanted was to go home, but Steve would always urge me to stay so he could push himself doing shots. I could see what a benefit my sobriety was to him—I'd become the designated driver.

For the very first time, I was seeing through sober eyes all of the dysfunction that existed within the movement. I no longer found the parties interesting. The tired conversations were boring, the booze-sodden words and actions really stupid. Had I really sounded like that? Pretty much everything they said seemed ridiculous to me now.

I began to see how each group's splintering was caused by infighting, the need for competition between members and entire crews. Each time a new crew formed, its values were one step further removed from the original goal. That sense of belonging I'd so desperately wanted, along with the desire for protection from my old friends Raymond, Isabelle, Brianna and Bentley, had prompted me, like many others, to jump from one crew to the next until I'd finally found myself with the Hammerskins. Perversely, it seemed as though "white unity" was impossible because of the infighting.

The more I searched, the more I realized there had never been any end goals, any sustainable causes in the groups and crews I'd belonged to. If white supremacists ever achieved their all-white society, I could see that they'd need to find the next big something to set them on fire. Like a lot of other movements, what the Hammerskins seemed to enjoy most was a reason to fight, an excuse to throw the first punch. Two good friends had died: Jan while carrying out illegal business and Corey, a one-time Hammerskin who'd taken his own life. The issue of bringing kids into a hate-filled environment had bothered me way more than I'd expected, and I couldn't understand how anyone could take advantage of Jan's mother's grief. I no longer agreed with any of the propaganda I'd been fed.

Some part of me now recognized that it was easier to be on my own in the world than to have to always earn my keep with the crew. I'd enjoyed feeling important in my first few years in white power — the titles of enforcer giving me an inflated sense of myself—but I no longer needed those. My life was better than it had been. I had a roof over me, a bed to sleep in every night, a family and a job I enjoyed. Even though I didn't know who I really was, I was content to be a nobody, a chick named Lauren. That was enough for me.

I'm sure some members could tell I was starting to pull away. I questioned everything and rarely engaged in conversations, preferring to sit off by myself at those parties I dragged myself to. Instead of telling Steve the truth, I used the excuse that some of his friends pissed me off, which they did. I knew he wouldn't want me to cut ties with the movement, not without a challenge, so I started making excuses to be around him less, telling him I couldn't hang out because I had plans.

I began to see that our relationship had always been boring, pretty much one-dimensional. In the beginning, when Steve and I first began dating, I thought he was good-looking, nice and level-headed, at least compared to the other guys I'd met. We had several things in common—the movement, music and tattoos—and the sex was good. But we didn't do much by ourselves other than go out for the odd lunch or dinner. Most weekends we'd hang out at his house watching TV shows like *Breaking Bad* or *Sons of Anarchy*. I never went to any of his work functions, he never came to any of mine. Sometimes I'd be invited to his parents' house for dinner; most of the time I'd sit quietly, feeling awkward and out of place, while his family—very nice people—talked around me. He didn't seem to like my old high school friends and the one time he accompanied me to a family get-together, he complained on the way home, "That one cousin of yours is a dumbass."

We rarely socialized with anyone who wasn't in the movement and Steve would shut me down if I suggested going away to the Caribbean or Europe. "I like it here."

"Don't you want to see other places?"

"No, not really."

For a white power member, it was bad enough to see people of other religions, races and cultures in your own city. God forbid you spend money to fly someplace heavily populated by them.

We hadn't spoken about kids at first, but when I went off to college, I started hearing about them more and more. Now it was finally clear to me how much Steve wanted them in his life. And how much I didn't. Arguing was ruining our sex life; I was losing interest in intimacy and Steve was having problems performing in bed.

One of the very last white power gatherings I attended began with me defending my sobriety to Steve, who'd pressured me to drink countless times before. "Maybe you don't have cirrhosis of the liver," he challenged. "Maybe you're not drinking because you're pregnant."

"How do you figure I'm pregnant when you can't even get it up?" I shot back, pleased with myself for embarrassing him in front of his friends, just as he'd done to me with his talk of having kids. I laughed inwardly but dreaded the drive home, knowing he'd be sitting in the passenger seat, grumpy, irritable, unwilling to listen to anything I said or take me seriously.

Soon after that last gathering, I visited a tattoo shop in Oshawa to inquire about removing my 1488 tattoo. Its meaning—we must secure the existence of our race and a future for white children—along with my frustration at having to defend myself time and time again, had been getting on my nerves. I was tired, fed up with seeing it in the mirror every day, more so now that I'd finally decided to leave the movement.

During my consultation, I was introduced to a really nice Indigenous woman who explained she'd be looking after me. "Why are you removing it?" she asked, examining my neck.

The irony was not lost on me. "I made some bad mistakes when I was young and I'm trying to get away from them now," I replied honestly.

"I'd love to help you with this," she answered, to my relief. I'd thought I might have to beg but, surprisingly, she offered me the treatments at a discount. "I believe everyone has good in them," she told me, "no matter how many bad things they've done."

She offered to start right away. I prided myself on my pain tolerance but, at the first zap of the laser, I yelled, "Motherfucker!" and nearly jumped from the chair. It felt like she was snapping an elastic band against my neck over and over again and, although I didn't give up, I was gripping the chair with everything I had.

She laughed as I squirmed. "I did warn you how much this would hurt, didn't I?" Not more than a minute later she said, "Alright, that's our first session done!"

When I looked in the mirror, I could see some serious fading already happening, even though the whole area was burnt to a crisp. I was pleased to see one of the 8s was nearly gone while the remaining numbers had lost significant amounts of pigment. Wow, I thought, This is so cool! I couldn't wait to see the end of the thing. Life had just become more peaceful, thanks to one very nice lady.

The first thing I did when I got home was show my mom my new and improved look. "Hey, look what I did to my tattoo," I sang, pointing at my neck. I knew she'd be overjoyed because she'd always hated how visible, how stark that tattoo was against my skin.

"Wow," she smiled, "there's some serious fading there."

I had wrestled with telling my mom about my growing distance from the movement, but I couldn't find the right words and my ego didn't want to admit she'd been right. This, at least, was a first step for both of us.

I wondered if Steve would be opposed to me removing the tattoo, but he wasn't. He'd once asked, "What if you were out in public by yourself? You could get beaten up," so I figured he wasn't too fond of it either.

During the summer of 2013, I began posting pictures of my faded 1488 tattoo on Facebook, knowing some of my family would be pleased while many contacts from the movement would not. Part of me hoped they'd be pissed enough to delete me—saving me the trouble of doing it myself—and some did. But one guy messaged me, demanding to know why I'd removed the tattoo. He wasn't affiliated with the Hammerskins but referred to himself as a white nationalist, one who hung out with "preppers," (also known as paranoia cases) people who trained and dug underground bunkers in their backyards in preparation for the impending race wars. I should have realized I'd get pushback from him; he'd previously tried to recruit me from the Hammerskins.

Rather than brushing him off, I made the mistake of getting into a long, draining discussion that ultimately went nowhere, something

I kept doing with people who'd once called me friend but who now called me traitor. One person asked: *How can you just throw away your European heritage like this?* to which I replied: *It's going to be the same as it is now. I'm just not wrapping my whole life around it anymore.* I really didn't understand my need to fight them on every little issue. Maybe I just enjoyed the arguing, maybe a part of me felt it would be easier to leave if I pissed them all off. Either way, I continued to fight and argue with them for several months before it too got really old.

I was mentally and emotionally exhausted. Fuck it, I finally told myself. Why should I have to justify myself to people I'd considered my friends once upon a time but who were no longer part of my world? I began blocking, deleting and ignoring incoming calls and messages. Why hadn't I thought of doing this before? I discovered what a relief it was not to have to deal with that shit anymore.

My job with Staszek came to an abrupt end when he fired me after about a year, telling me his wife had accused him of having an affair with me. While he had never touched me inappropriately, the harassment had been constant and at some point, I had started thinking, This guy's a pervert. This isn't normal. A boss shouldn't be behaving this way to an employee.

I'd needed the job, so I'd sucked it up, rebuffing his advances. I knew he was angry that I'd pushed him away repeatedly, and now, suddenly, his wife was jealous? I questioned how much of that was true. There were times when I considered revenge, moments when I wanted to send his wife screenshots of his texts asking me to have sex with him, texts that continued even after I left his workplace. But I recognized he was just another pain in my ass, not worthy of my time any longer. Clearly, it was time for me to leave that part of my life behind too.

Staszek still owed me money so one day I drove to his workshop and walked in the unlocked door. I was polite but firm. "Can I have what I'm owed?"

Surprisingly, he didn't put up a fight. "I can't afford to give you the full amount," he began, digging into his pocket, "but here's what I have."

"That's fine," I said, turning to leave.

He caught up to me, cornering me far from the door. "My wife doesn't have to know about this."

"No," I said. He kept hounding me and I kept saying no until he blurted out, "I'll give you an extra hundred dollars if you do."

"Fuck off," I finally yelled. "Get out of my way." He wouldn't move, kept pleading with me even when I screamed, "NO!"

I tried repeatedly to get past him, but he was bigger than me and immovable. Finally, I hit him in the throat with my fist, stunning him. In that second, a customer opened the door and Staszek turned away abruptly, pretending he was actually working. I took off as quickly as I could. On the drive home, I couldn't help shaking as various scenarios, none of them good, played in my head.

I decided my next career choice should involve working someplace other than privately owned cabinetmaking shops. While I weighed my options, I accepted a volunteer position with Habitat for Humanity, driving around Durham Region picking up household donations with an upbeat guy named James. At first, I know I was standoffish; I was trying to shed the old "movement" version of myself but I was also fearful the process would make me too vulnerable, opening up old wounds I'd rather leave closed or exposing emotions I'd long buried. I had a hard time trusting people, mostly because of the promised brotherhood that hadn't come true but also because of the bullshit I'd endured while at the shelters. But James was incredibly warm and welcoming, a huge grin lighting up his face as he shook my hand. Anything but soft-spoken, James was my height and wore glasses. Talkative and friendlier than anyone I'd ever met, he was only a few years older than me but had already been through his own issues.

Right away, he dropped his guard. "I live with bipolar disorder."
I was dumbfounded. I'd never met anyone so open before.
Hesitatingly I told him a little of my past and was amazed when he
didn't judge me. For the four months we worked together, we provided one another with free therapy. I found it refreshing to spend
hours each day with someone who didn't want to argue, didn't force
his opinions on me and didn't make me feel defensive. As he shared
his views on healthy relationships, it started me wondering, How do I
get something like that?

When an ad appeared on TV for a website called loveisrespect.
org, I pulled up their page, reading with interest about consent and
respect within relationships, something I'd never experienced. Steve
had never beaten or abused me, but neither had he stopped making
the comments about kids that bothered me so much, long after I'd
asked him to stop. I knew I'd never have a healthy relationship with
him and finally understood that that was what I was searching for.

Over the span of a year, I had six more laser treatments on my neck
tattoo; with less ink to erase each time, the pain gradually lessened
enough for me to make jokes while gripping the chair. As my tattoo
slowly disappeared, I continued to disengage from the toxic lifestyle
I'd lived for the last five years.

The process of leaving white power was draining and my last two
years with the Hammerskins, from Jan's death in March 2012 until
the summer of 2014, were a chore. I'd often receive harassing calls or
messages from members demanding I stay and wanting to get into
long debates, none of which were ever constructive.

"Are you still white power?" one asked.

"No."

"What do you mean, no?"

"I just don't care for it anymore."

"You're not out partying with Negros are you?"

When the laser specialist finished zapping my neck at the last session, I asked her, "How's it look?"

"Pretty damned good," she laughed.

No traces of the numbers remained beneath the redness and irritation. Days later, once the scarring had faded, all I could see was the faint outline of the 4. Nothing else. I was no longer a walking billboard; my five-year monstrosity was gone. I was pleased that my ultimate goal—eliminating the questions and symbols of my time in the movement—had been achieved. The tattoo was no longer a reflection of who I was.

Steve's only remark was, "I'd never have been able to guess it was there." I think he was smart enough to realize the tattoo removal was part of my separation from the group, but we rarely discussed it. I had originally wanted him to leave the movement with me, but he wanted, just as much, to pull me back into it. "Why do you want to leave anyway?"

"'Cause this is fucking stupid," I'd reply, ticked off by his question and attitude. He offered no support at all. To get him back I'd say, "Oh, you going to your cult meeting?"

"It's not a cult," he'd huff. "It's a political movement."

I continued detaching from him, rarely approaching him for help in my everyday life or telling him what I was up to. One day I asked him what he would do if I found out I wasn't one hundred percent white.

"I'd tell you I couldn't be with you anymore," he said.

I'd thrown that question at him thinking a DNA test could be an easy way out of our relationship and the group, even though I was fairly sure I came from European stock. But, as we saw less and less of each other, our relationship was ending all by itself. And I was fine with that.

I decided to apply to the Carpenters' Union; acceptance required completing a six-week, entry-level course. I easily passed the basic math and English tests, but the rest was a struggle, in part because of the lingering effects of the brain injury I'd acquired from my 2009 beating. At the age of twenty-four, my short-term memory and focus sucked. I'd had problems with the book-learning while at Humber; in order to retain anything I'd had to read the page over and over again. Taking in the teachers' instruction was also hard and by the end of a day's lessons I often felt like a complete idiot. I was embarrassed to be having the same troubles this time around but I carried on working hard and was offered a job with a scaffolding company in Toronto as soon as I finished.

My first workday was the following Monday and, like a rookie, I showed up at the site—a natural gas plant in Toronto—with a huge bag of tools. I didn't know what to bring so I'd packed everything I had. Luckily, the foreman and my coworker didn't rip on me for acting like a newbie but instead showed me the work I'd be doing and chatted and joked with me, leaving me feeling pretty happy by day's end.

The following day, two others joined us on site, both Black guys. Thank God that stupid neck tattoo was gone. One of them shared my interest in music and, by sharing some lyrics he'd written, rekindled my interest for the first time in years. We told countless dirty jokes and I was reminded of my college friend Shemar. I couldn't wrap my head around the fact that a year ago I would have written these guys off because of my white power beliefs and irrational fears. I enjoyed their company so much more than that of any of the friends I'd left behind.

Meanwhile, I caught word that the Hammerskins were hatching a plan to target a group of Black guys at a bar in my hometown "because they're hanging out there." I was hoping Steve wouldn't get involved, but I knew that, against his better judgment, he would. He was one of the crew, so of course he'd go along with them. I knew about the plan but I didn't know the targets and, much as I now felt it was wrong, I wouldn't have tipped them off anyway. That would have meant narking on my boyfriend and possibly getting myself into trouble with his crew. In the end, the Black guys never showed up, but it was a clear signal that I couldn't continue to live in both worlds.

That July, Steve and I went to his family cottage one last time. It was just the two of us and, since we hadn't seen each other in a month, I thought it would be a nice getaway—right up until he brought up kids. I shut down immediately.

Steve noticed. "Are you mad?" he asked.

"Yes."

"I'm just bringing up the subject of kids to see if you'd be open to it," he explained.

"How many fucking times do I need to say no for you to understand?" I asked in frustration. "Either you aren't taking me seriously or you're trying to turn me into your ideal housewife and incubator."

"Hey, let's forget about this and go to the beach."

Stubbornly, I said, "I don't want to."

When he saw how serious I was, we decided to pack up our stuff and drive back to his place, where I'd left my car. The drive was long and silent, with me texting someone else the entire time and Steve pouting because he didn't get his way.

By the time we got back, we agreed our relationship was over. "This was a really hard decision to make," Steve said as we stood in his driveway. I didn't respond because, for me, it hadn't been difficult at all. It had been inevitable.

As I got into the car, he leaned down and requested, "Just so I'm clear, would you only date white guys after this?"

At some point along the highway I realized I wasn't grieving the five-year relationship I'd just left behind. It was as if I'd lost a casual friend, an acquaintance, nothing more. I felt a profound sense of relief. I was looking forward to being on my own, having some casual flings—with both guys and girls—to see what the universe had in store for my future.

I'm free! I sang on my way home that night. Free!

JEANETTE

When Lauren first decided to erase her tattoo, I didn't realize it represented her disillusionment with the movement. I simply assumed she was sick of the unwanted attention. I'd heard her shrug away questions, mumbling something about it being a mistake she'd made when she was younger, hoping the person asking would be satisfied and leave her alone. I had watched her struggle to hide the 1488 beneath makeup, bandanas, collars or her long hair, and so was overjoyed to see it disappearing. How ironic was it that, without it, she would be free to apply for work anywhere without fearing retribution or discrimination.

I had no idea how far removed she was from white power by then, even though we now spoke freely about most other things going on in her life. She'd often share stories about her workday, the guys she met on site, her friends James and Marco and events happening in their lives but, as I still refused to talk about the movement, Lauren kept most of the Hammerskin stuff to herself.

She did share with me their push for her to have kids, which she wanted no part of. After white power parties, Lauren would rant about their "jokes." Rolo, in particular, used to bug her constantly about getting pregnant, even though he and his wife had no kids of their own. Lauren often recounted his pushy comments, her frustration boiling over when it happened time and time again. Since leaving Staszek's shop, she'd become more like the old Lauren, the daughter I'd known before her father died, asking for my opinions, bouncing ideas off me and wanting to spend time talking. One night, while we were sitting in her room chatting, she asked my opinion about Rolo's obsession with her getting pregnant. "Well," I suggested, "I'd say you have two choices. Tell Rolo to screw himself in front of everyone or just don't go to the parties." I knew it was never that simple but I wanted to encourage her to stand up for herself.

We also discussed, at length, Steve's preoccupation with children. Because he was older and stable, I'd always thought of Steve as mature but I began to wonder if he was as much a victim of the white power mentality and ideology as Lauren. Was he drawn to the movement because of the feelings of power and entitlement it gave him? Or because it was a comfortable rut? Did he really want children? Or was it a way for him to fit in with the Hammerskins? He loved the *idea* of children as a means to continue the race and his family name, but probably hadn't considered the long-term ramifications of becoming a parent.

Eventually Lauren shared her reasons for quitting drinking. To say I was relieved isn't enough. My father had been a heavy drinker for most of his life and another family member struggled with alcohol so I was pleased, in a strange way, that her body had forced her to give up her partying ways. I could see it wasn't easy; despite her strong will she was dependent on alcohol to give her courage, to help her don a protective mask to cover her insecurities. Maybe even deal with those she called friends. She'd come home from a weekend with Steve, grumpy and irritable, complaining about the pressure she was under to drink, but she stuck to her decision to abstain.

Just as I had during Lauren's elementary and high school days, I found myself counselling her before and after weekends away. Her frustration was apparent, her anger at being pressured into things she wasn't comfortable with obvious, even without her speaking them aloud. I could see she was outgrowing the Hammerskins and what I considered their reprehensible beliefs, juvenile ideals and boyhood fantasies of ruling the world, so I did what I could to encourage her to speak up for herself until she was ready to leave the movement for good.

Still, I was puzzled when Lauren called one evening to say she was returning early from Steve's cottage. "Why? I thought you were staying the whole weekend?"

"Steve and I are done. I've had enough of him pressuring me to have kids and go back to the movement."

I was saddened but not really surprised. As much as I'd thought of him as a future son-in-law—a stable, responsible young man who owned a house and held down a good job, unlike the other creeps Lauren had dated—he didn't seem too worried about Lauren's mental health, misgivings or lack of interest in having a family. When she arrived home, we sat down and talked and I finally understood what had happened, how she'd outgrown their relationship. Viewing the world through more mature eyes, she'd begun understanding the people around her, eventually becoming secure in herself, her work and her plans for the future. Now she needed time on her own to find the life she deserved.

In July 2015, my father quietly passed away from cancer. We hadn't seen or spoken to him since Paul's funeral eight years before. He'd made my mother's life miserable since disowning us, refusing to have me and my children in his house or at family gatherings, not speaking to her if she spent time with us, even threatening divorce when she visited Paul in hospital. He had even tried to stop his youngest sister from seeing me when she visited from England.

We'd made our peace with my father's choice to exclude us years before and attended his celebration of life only to support my mother. We had grieved when he'd made his earlier decision but felt nothing now and shed no tears. In fact, as I watched my brothers struggle with their emotions, I felt detached, far removed from the entire proceeding. My father had made it abundantly clear years before that we were dead to him. Now, thankfully, his own death had freed us from his bitterness and hate, just as Lauren had finally freed herself from the Hammerskins. We were both ready to move on.

CHAPTER EIGHTEEN

The Void

LAUREN _____

There's a void left in your life when you exit the white power scene. You've wrapped your entire identity around the movement, its beliefs and edicts. When you detach from everything you've lived and preached for so long, you start to question who you are.

Rebuilding my life wasn't easy. Perhaps the hardest part was shedding the veneer, the shield, the false sense of power I'd worn for years. Losing my dad had left me feeling alone and vulnerable; I'd donned a mask, a barrier born of anger and unfairness that had allowed me to be drawn into white power, which in turn had become an outlet for my rage. I now had to accept the fact that my outer image couldn't keep me safe, that it did the complete opposite, bringing trouble I'd never had before joining the movement.

There were times when I was tempted to go back out of loneliness, when I longed for my old friends and that brotherhood they'd promised. Intellectually, I knew I'd never truly belonged in extremism but my emotional self couldn't let go of that notion. I knew I wouldn't feel appreciated, as if I was part of something, but I still wanted to find that feeling somewhere. It took a long time to see that I had to find myself in order to fully let go of the movement and the resentment I held towards ex-friends. Just as I'd learned, while growing up, to ignore what I didn't want to see, I knew I'd have to dissociate from everything I'd once been.

Holding in that resentment and anger wasn't helping me move forward so I turned to meditation, something that allowed me quiet time to be honest with myself, with no distractions. YouTube and Facebook were filled with meditation demos; I'd try one, then another, until I found a few that worked for me, discovering that meditation isn't as complicated as people say it is. I would find a quiet place, close my eyes, focus on my breathing and acknowledge any thoughts that passed through my head, using incense to help me relax. Acknowledge the thought but don't buy into it. Simple. It wasn't a quick fix but it was helpful and there were times when I'd have epiphanies when I'd be better able to process my past. My biggest insight was that my white power life was an obstacle I'd thrown in my own path, that I couldn't blame it on anyone else.

Working in interior finishing and scaffolding gave me the long overdue self-esteem and confidence I had been desperately looking for. The friends I reconnected with supported me fully and I made new friends at work, people of all different backgrounds. I met many women my age who weren't gossipy or two-faced like those I'd gone to school with, a very nice surprise. But unwanted thoughts and negative programming, I soon learned, can linger a long time after the physical involvement is over. I'd see someone of colour and my thoughts would instantly return to racial slurs that now horrified me but seemed impossible to purge. Accepting friendships with people who weren't white, who didn't look like me was difficult at first. The whole year I was at college with Shemar, I couldn't shake the "n-word"—it would pop into my head immediately, as soon as I saw him. It was the same with some of the guys I worked with now. They were great people but at first my years of indoctrination wouldn't let me forget they were Black. How could I think those things about friends? I felt terrible about it, especially when they were cool about accepting me into their lives.

Each time I saw a woman with a baby, I'd remember the shaming I'd been subjected to. Some of my new friends, mostly women dating guys I knew, were mothers themselves and I found it hard to connect with them. I'm sure I lost a few friendships because of my discomfort but I also got to know some really cool parents who were supportive as I struggled to turn my life around, and I was grateful that many of them didn't judge me for my earlier choices. I began to see what healthy relationships looked like, how they were created and nurtured by two people using equality, communication and compromise.

I had to change the hardwiring in my own head. Searching the internet, I found some information on critical thinking, the ability to make judgments and form opinions based on observable facts and empirical research, discounting personal biases. Critical thinking skills allowed me to ask myself, Do any of those old thoughts make sense? I'd recall Donny's words, "They're out to get us," and realize how little supportive evidence there had been to back them up. No one had ever asked me to apologize for being white. There was no reason to fear or hate anyone, no reason to think they were out to get me. I was the one out to get myself.

No one in the white power groups I'd belonged to, I realized, had had my back as they'd promised. As I let go of all that disappointment and hatred, I was surprised at how many people outside the movement did, in fact, have my back. I now understood why my mom and brother had called the police when I'd cut contact with them—they'd been concerned about me, something I couldn't see at the time because of my preoccupation with the movement and its disdain for my middle-class family. My mom and brother had offered their absolute love and acceptance, even though I probably didn't deserve them. When I began opening up to my mom, I asked why she'd accepted me back so easily and she told me, "That's part of loving your child. When they want to change, the door has to be open." Even some of my dad's family showed support. I felt hugely disconnected from them at first but slowly they started speaking to me, treating me as an equal. Eventually I opened up, and things got easier when I could freely admit I'd been wrong.

Critical thinking helped me acknowledge and appreciate the many good people of colour who had passed through my life: the two Black guys, supposed enemies of white power, who'd helped Raymond and me after our drunken brawl; my college friend, Shemar—once I let my guard down and got to know him, I could never hate him; the guys I've worked with, funny, warm, decent people who just happen to have dark skin. I began to see how I'd separated black people into two groups: those I knew and therefore liked, and those I'd never met and so could freely hate.

So, who really was the "enemy?" The other group members were only partially responsible. I'd chosen to join in the rallies and gatherings, the rhetoric and hate. I'd created my own narratives about society, gradually buying into the fear before blindly burying myself in it. The drinking, the movement, the senseless choices were all things I'd done because I hadn't wanted to look deep inside myself for answers. I'd been my own worst enemy.

One night I received a message from a former friend, older than me, not a patched Hammerskin but one who'd been loosely tied to the group: *I've left the movement as well. I was wondering if you'd like to meet up?*

Sure, I replied, not surprised to hear of someone else leaving. I drove to his place in Newmarket, but when I pulled into the parking lot of his apartment building I saw three other familiar faces staring at me out of the darkness. Immediately I closed the car window, locked the doors and stomped on the gas pedal, ripping out of the lot as fast as I could. Goddamit! I screamed at myself. What did that just do to my car? How I could have been taken in so easily? What a stupid mistake. Arriving home, shaken and upset, I made sure to block my phone, so no one from the movement could reach me again.

A year out of the movement, I still carried a knife when I left the house, mostly out of fear of meeting my old "friends." I wouldn't start a fight, but I still chose to conceal a weapon on my body, just in case.

Funnily enough, rather than allaying my fears, the knife made them worse. I was buying into the fear of running into someone simply by carrying the knife, so in 2015 I locked it away in a box. It took some getting used to, not having it with me, but in the end I felt better.

I continued to receive online threats and harassing messages. "Go fuck yourself," were the first words I heard when I picked up the phone one night. "You're a traitor."

"Dude," I replied, "That's not an insult to me anymore."

Another guy called saying, "You'll be the first one hung on the Day of the Rope," a reference to the novel *The Turner Diaries* where race traitors would be murdered together on the same day. Some of their words wounded, but they also reminded me how tired I had become of the drama that existed within white power circles: fistfights, competition to be on top, meaningless rhetoric, drinking too much. I knew these taunts would never escalate beyond the computer screen. And that, thankfully, I could switch off.

For the next couple of years, I worked in construction and worked on myself—working hard to understand who I had been and who I would be going forward, making new friends and finding new interests. A family friend introduced me to alcohol ink painting; I enjoyed having a hobby and loved showing off my finished artwork.

I had hoped to enjoy my newly single life in peace, but my mom kept bugging me to date. At her insistence, I tried online dating, but it was a waste of time, a colossal disappointment. One guy played head games with me, asking me what insecurities I had. "Why does that matter?"

"I just need to know these things," he replied.

Another guy couldn't even hold a conversation during the date but once I got home, he texted me asking for nude photos. I just wasn't interested in the guys on the dating sites and got more defensive each time my mom brought the subject up. During one conversation, as my mother watched me tapping on my phone—"Who are you texting? Is it a boy?" —I let slip that I was bisexual. "Men aren't the only ones on my radar." I covered the subsequent pause with, "Listen, with the number of dumb things I've done, this should be the least of your concerns."

She seemed to have a hard time accepting my admission, which made me angry. Once again, I asked myself, do I really belong here? Do I have a place in this family? When she started lecturing me about dating again, saying, "It's going to be weird if you bring home girls," it only made things worse.

In the spring of 2016, almost two years after I had left the movement, Caleb, the guy I'd met at Paul Fromm's meeting years before, contacted me out of the blue. He had hung out with the Canadian Hammerskins briefly after he was released from prison but too many disagreements had stopped him from coming around. *How are you doing?*

Doing well. Just working. I'm out of the movement, just so you know.

The movement in Canada isn't a healthy environment for anyone. He explained how he'd suffered from mental health issues most of his life, but that his current poor state of mind was due to his ex-girlfriend's having had an abortion without his consent. We continued texting for several days. He said he wasn't in the group anymore and that the "idiots" we'd hung out with were pretty toxic. I figured he was on the road to change, just as I was, but didn't know how to actually ask him. Maybe I was scared to hear his answer. I clung to the hope that other people could change just I had and wanted to help him if I could, but what if Caleb wasn't ready?

I agreed to meet up and hang out for the evening as friends. He talked endlessly about his ex, the abortion and their split; I was pro-choice but listened politely because the incident mattered to him and, frankly, I found his "injured bird" attitude sort of appealing. We didn't discuss the movement, even though I could see hate tattoos prominently displayed on his biceps. I knew how expensive it was to have them removed and assumed from what he didn't say that he was leaving or had already left the movement.

We talked mostly about him but one thing I did get into was my reason for quitting drinking. "Good for you," he said when I'd finished explaining my liver problem.

After three weeks of texting, Caleb admitted he wanted to date me. Having someone to text and talk with made me feel a little less lonely. I wasn't really attracted to him but I liked the idea of having someone to hang out with and I enjoyed our conversations, so I said, "Sure. I'll give it a try. But I would like to take things slowly."

My idea of taking it slow was to have fun and hang out for a bit until we knew each other better. On our first date I drove to his place in Toronto, parking in his building's underground, and discovered Caleb's idea of going slow was to tell me to "get those clothes off" minutes after we'd cuddled on his bed. He heard my boundaries as, "Take the relationship slowly but let's jump into bed right away."

Some part of me wanted to get laid, but not on the first date. His anti-abortion and anti-birth control stance scared me, and the sexual assault attempts I'd endured made me defensive. I was filled with fear and found it hard to trust him, but I couldn't get to my car without his access key. When his hands reached for my pants, my brain shut off, as if I wasn't even there. Numbly, I took off my T-shirt, knowing that was what was expected.

I never came right out and asked Caleb if he was still white power but over the next few weeks, it became clear that he still held those beliefs, even though he wasn't part of any group. He'd rant about the Jews' control of the media, discuss the notion of white genocide and use the N-bomb as if it meant nothing to him. When I invited him to our house for the May long weekend, the only time he met my brother and mother, he spent an hour that Sunday morning trying to shove his opinions down their throats.

Every time he spoke, I shut down more and more before finally admitting to myself that he was never going to change. For him, I was someone to pass the time with while he tried to forget his ex. So it wasn't a surprise that our relationship, volatile and unsatisfactory, only lasted a few months. We split less than two weeks after his visit to Whitby when he called to rage at me for some perceived slight, behaviour I had already warned him about. I was done with subservient relationships. He didn't take it very well, texting and calling, trying to convince me to come back in one breath, then ripping on me for leaving him in the next.

With Caleb gone, I spent my free time working and meditating, things I should have focused on all along. I also started writing, another technique for processing my past. I wrote a short, rather vague piece that had popped into my head while meditating one day —"Black, white, grey, blue, green, purple, I could care less now. Even those with a sketchy past, obviously I can not judge them at all..I only look at who someone is in this present moment."—and summoned the courage to search for an online forum. I emailed Anti-Racist Canada, the hate-watch site that had tracked me once upon a time, explaining that I wanted to share my story, to get out the message that it is possible to leave. The main contact was surprisingly friendly. She replied: *You were always a bit of an odd duck to us. It didn't seem like you really belonged in that movement at times. Our consensus back then was that you could do better.*

Wow. Even those I'd perceived as enemies back then had seen through me and wished a better future for me. For the next week or two we chatted via email, until eventually my piece was published on their blog.

Caleb called. The minute I picked up the phone he began yelling and talking down to me. "How could you do this?" he ranted. "Reaching out to Anti-Racist Canada? Don't you know what they're about? They're against our people."

"You and I are not together anymore. I can do whatever the hell I want. You have no say in what I do. You never should have."

"You never had much to stand on when you were in the movement," he shot back, "because you hung out with the Vinland Hammerskin guys. Those motherfuckers know nothing; it's easy to be white power when you live in the suburbs of Toronto."

Fed up, I said, "You know what you should do instead of attacking me? Find a job and stop playing the victim." Then I hung up. For two days straight, he texted me, trying to prove his point, telling me he'd never speak to me again. I couldn't take him seriously and finally, I texted: *Everything you've said sounds like utter bullshit. If you don't want to talk to me, I'd suggest you start doing just that.* I heard nothing more from him but blocked him on every digital platform I could think of, just in case. Some guys aren't that easy to get rid of.

In the summer of 2016, in addition to my full-time job, I began volunteering as an admin assistant for EMHARS (Eating Disorders, Mental Health, Addiction Recovery Support), a Facebook support group. I enjoyed helping people, so I was asked to run the forum, answering users' questions, sharing small parts of my former life and counselling those who needed someone to talk to. There must have been over a hundred people actively looking for help and probably ten admin workers like me who posted supportive messages and provided assistance when needed.

One I became friends with was Justin, a peer support worker in the field of mental health and addictions recovery who was also volunteering his time. I was impressed by how much he knew and how friendly he was when messaging. At first, our chats revolved around substance abuse. Then we spent hours chatting, making "That's what she said" jokes—I wasn't really professional with anyone, an approach that seemed to work for me—and eventually talking about ourselves. I had no idea how he would respond when he learned of my extremist past. Turns out I needn't have worried, he held no judgments.

Late that summer, my mom, brother and I flew to the United Kingdom for a vacation, travelling through England and Scotland for two weeks, connecting with our heritage and relatives in southwest England. Before we'd even left the chaos that is Toronto's Pearson International Airport, my mom quietly commented on the vast array of multicultural people around us. I responded, "Oh, you mean all the Pakis?" Another mental glitch. After more than two years, I was still fighting to reprogram my brain.

The flight seemed endless, especially as I'd gone more than eight hours without a cigarette by the time we landed at London's Heathrow Airport. Along with that, I was nervous about clearing customs with my criminal record. I worried needlessly, it turns out, because the customs officer stamped my passport and said, "Enjoy your stay."

Our first few days were spent exploring London's architecture and history, something I couldn't enjoy without the niggling sense of shame that came with having been in a hate movement modelled on Nazi Germany. It turned out I wasn't as proud of my involvement as I'd once claimed to be because I found myself thinking, If I'd had genuine pride, I wouldn't have joined a neo-fascist group, wouldn't have ignored my British heritage and all of this beauty.

One day, when I stepped outside of a museum for a cigarette, I was approached by a guy who asked, "Hey, can I bum one off you?" I gave him the smoke, noticing for the first time his boots with white laces and his T-shirt displaying an iron eagle. As we talked, he noticed my accent and asked where I was from.

"Canada."

"Oh, Canadistan," he replied with a laugh. I'd heard the term before and knew exactly where it was coming from but held back my comments on his boots and shirt. "It's a shame when countries and history go to waste," he continued. "All that beauty right down the drain."

I stopped him, showing him where I'd sported the 1488 tattoo. "Hey, um, look at the side of my neck. I lasered off the 1488 that used to be here."

"Why'd you remove it?"

"Because," I explained, "I left the white power movement behind."

He didn't seem to know how to respond and I was hesitant to tell him more. After all, I'd become a traitor. I'd walked away. "Listen, man, I don't hold a grudge towards you. I just hope you can come to terms with whatever drove you here in the first place." Extending my hand, I smiled. "I gotta go, but it was nice chatting with you. Best of luck."

I'd always wondered how I'd react if I met someone still involved in hate. Would I knock them out? Debate them? Until the moment he smiled and shook my hand, my questions had gone un-answered. Now, armed with the confidence to be myself, I knew my future approach would be non-aggressive, compassionate and straightforward.

I had finally come to the conclusion that I'd been the one to throw barriers in my life's path and it was up to me to remove them. So I agreed to be a guest speaker at Justin's place of work, offering my perspectives on recovery. As a bonus, I would finally get to meet him in person.

It was a small group, so I wasn't too nervous and didn't even rehearse what I was going to say. While his boss was introducing me, I told myself, Keep the language clean, don't swear. But it made no difference. I still managed to drop a few F-bombs. Luckily, no one seemed to mind. If anything, they needed to hear an authentic voice, not a bland and well-rehearsed speech.

I began with, "Hi everyone. I'm Lauren. To date, I have four and a half years of sobriety." I didn't get to finish before they started clap-ping. It's commonplace for recovery groups to do that when a speaker recounts their "clean time," but I wasn't used to such praise.

I laughed. "Guys, let me finish. Alright, let's get on with the rest of this. I'm also a former extremist gang member who spent time on the streets."

The audience remained engaged for the entire time I spoke. At one point I noticed a guy nodding and staring off as if in self-reflection. Good. That was what I wanted. To strike some nerves in people, to get them thinking. Once finished, I received a round of applause and tons of questions, which made me feel great.

"Do you feel like those beatings you took made you tougher?" one man asked.

His question made sense to me. I'd often told people, "Beatings toughen you up," something I'd truly believed at the time. Since getting out, I'd learned that walking away actually toughens you up.

"Honestly, no. It taught me to choose my friends a little more carefully. I thought I was tough shit but the reality is, even though I still live with the lingering effects of that beating, I needed that knock to my ego. That's not to say violence is the solution," I cautioned. "It might seem like it at the time, but it gets you nowhere fast."

Justin and I soon became a couple, our relationship healthy and enjoyable. My prior relationships had taught me what I didn't want, and with him there was none of the garbage I'd come to expect from guys. I know he won't spout verbal abuse like Raymond and, unlike Steve, he respects what I have to say. His only expectation is that I be loyal to him.

Justin enjoys adventure as much as I do, and we create memories by zip-lining, taking in the CN Tower Edge Walk and whitewater rafting. He's not a metalhead like me but he's willing to go to metal and punk rock concerts and encourages me to get into the mosh pit and go nuts. He holds my backpack and guards my dearest possession—a blanket my father bought me on a family trip to Sudbury, Ontario, that I'd kept with me while on the streets. It's the only thing I've never misplaced, never had stolen. And unlike other people who know of it, he never makes fun of me for keeping it close.

JEANETTE

Lauren's victory over her inner demons was accomplished surprisingly quietly. There was none of the drama we'd come to expect from her, none of the screaming or stomping that had characterized her descent into the movement. She worked diligently, spending time with her meditation stones, incense and singing bowls, all of which were new to our home and way of thinking. The singing bowls, in particular, drove my son crazy—closing his door, he'd put on headphones and crank up his music to shut out the strange vibrations sailing down the hall. I found the stones intriguing and often asked her what each was for.

Lauren became a wonderful, caring member of the family, willing to sit and talk, to listen and consider points of view that weren't her own. Neither my mother nor I had to tiptoe around her, concerned that a wrong phrase could set off her temper, a definite relief from those early years after Paul's death. Religion, politics, sex—you name it, everything was freely and joyfully discussed around our dinner table. Even Lauren's face became open and curious, not closed off and mulishly set as it had been for so long. I could see the glow of pride in my mom's eyes when she looked at her granddaughter, now a happy, funny, open adult whose company she could enjoy. I credited Lauren's meditation for some of that, but mostly I believe she was ready to change.

When Lauren and Steve split, I assumed she was out of the movement's clutches, safe and sound, ready to either resume her old life or start building a new one. I encouraged her to date and go out with friends, hoping she'd meet a variety of people, perhaps create a caring circle to replace the people who'd disappointed her so. I pushed for her to date, worried she'd mope around the house, feeling as though she'd never meet anyone again, but I eased off after the first few failed attempts. It seemed as though everyone she met had their own agenda, an unhealthy atmosphere for someone still trying to claim her place in the world. I had no idea she'd carried a knife with her when she left the house, that she feared retribution, but she did share some of the hateful messages she received. We made time to talk through them.

Much as I wanted Lauren to date, finding out she was bisexual threw me. I'd never witnessed her interest in other girls and the topic of homosexuality hadn't often come up at the dinner table. I'd never thought to discuss it with my kids; now I had to rethink a lot of things, including my image of her future. I knew grandchildren weren't in the cards, but I struggled a bit with the idea of her being with a woman. Mostly I worried about how she'd be perceived in a world where bisexuality is still somewhat taboo. Feeling like an outsider had led her to white power; how would she handle the stigma of bisexuality? But then I realized that, as an adult, she's entitled to enjoy the life she wants without fear of recrimination. And my job is to support her, no matter what.

I was pleased when Lauren started seeing Caleb, asking general questions—where did you meet, where does he live, what does he do—never realizing he was connected to the movement. As Lauren's birthday falls around Victoria Day, I invited him to stay for the long weekend so we could all go out for dinner to celebrate. Caleb was engaging at first, discussing music and current events and participating in our teasing banter. He seemed to genuinely like Lauren.

Things changed the following morning when he cornered me at the breakfast table, spouting his opinions for over an hour and a half while Lauren sat by, helpless to stop him. "I get shit done in my building because I'm a Freemason," he bragged. Five minutes later he said, "They've found evidence that white people existed in North America before the Aboriginals." And later it was, "It's a Jewish conspiracy. Damned Jews are in control, they marry off their women to kings to gain influence in Europe." The minute he stopped for breath, I suggested they both go out for a while. I looked at my son after they left, the shock on his face mirroring mine. What the hell was that?

Throughout the day, I kept reflecting on Caleb's speech. The more I thought about it the more I realized I knew nothing of him, nothing of the values and beliefs he, Steve and Lauren had held. I'd always told myself they were "white power-lite," on the fringes of the movement, more interested in partying and blaming others for their problems than actually spreading their ideology. It shook me to hear the passion in Caleb's voice, his dedication to white power, to forwarding hate.

It seemed as though Lauren had fallen into a familiar pattern out of loneliness, dating Caleb more out of habit than real interest. He was a known entity, someone who delivered well-rehearsed speeches she'd heard many times before. I began to worry he'd pull her back into the muddy waters of extremism just by the force of his personality and spent that day fretting, dissecting Caleb's words with my son. "Did I hear him right?" I'd ask incredulously. "Was he trying to indoctrinate me? Was he really spouting white power shit?" The following morning—thank goodness both of them were out most of the previous day—I took my tea and newspaper out to the front porch, sitting quietly until Lauren told me she was driving Caleb to the train station. It was all I could do to be civil to him. I certainly didn't say, "I hope you'll come again" as I would have to any of her other friends.

When Lauren returned, I sat her down in my room and asked what I'd been too dumbstruck to ask earlier. "Who the hell is he? How do you know him?"

"I met him before, at one of our meetings."

"Did you know he was still in the movement?" I asked.

"He told me he'd left the group," Lauren replied with an uncertain shrug. "But I guess he hasn't left the beliefs behind."

With each answer I had more questions, more concerns, until I finally said, "I love you and I want you to feel free to have friends stay, but I can't have him in my house again." I was worried about how she'd take my criticisms of Caleb and my hard stance against his presence in her life and our house, but she surprised me by listening, considering my comments and questions in an adult manner. She apologized for his rant during breakfast and reassured me I'd never have to see him again. A far cry from how she'd responded years earlier.

Later that night, I googled Caleb. Holy shit! We'd had a convicted killer in our midst. The more I read the more frightened I became, not just for us but for my daughter's safety. I called Lauren into my room and pointed to the computer screen.

"Did you know about this?"

She had the grace not to lie but was slow with details. I could see she hadn't considered the impact this scumbag could have on her life—the potential loss of a good job and her widening circle of friends, not to mention her newly-built, shaky connections with family. I made it clear she deserved better. It was time she stopped collecting damaged people, falling for their fake "woe is me" lines. She'd been in limbo for too long—from shy, awkward Aaron, to Austin, the autistic boy she'd befriended at sixteen, to her drinking buddies, to Connor who wanted to impress his ex, to those connected to white power—every relationship seemed more about what she could do for them and less about what she received in return. Since Paul's death, I felt she'd been depending on the energy of others to feed her spunk, build her identity or drive her life forward. She needed to figure out who she was and then find someone who could stand on his—or her—own two feet.

In true mom form, I nagged Lauren to date Justin after hearing his name time and time again. There'd been no promising candidates since her split from Steve, who'd been, in a material sense at least, the model son-in-law (if owning a house and working full-time counted for anything). With each unsuitable first date or departure by ghosting I worried she was becoming jaded, fed up and ready to drop the dating scene altogether but, to her credit, she kept trying—yet another sign of her growing maturity.

At first, conversations were peppered with jokes Lauren and Justin shared. She'd tell me, "He's the male version of me," to which I'd groan mockingly, "Oh, my gosh, is the world ready for two of you?" Pretty soon, she was spending hours messaging with him, something she rarely did with any of her other friends. What, I asked repeatedly, did she have to lose by dating him?

Both my son and I adore Justin; he is gentle, kind, loving and devoted to Lauren, which is all I could ever ask for. He supports her, understands where she's been and encourages her to think outside the sometimes black-and-white parameters she still hasn't shaken. Their relationship is that of adults, one that includes bad times as well as good, and their eagerness to try new things together is wonderful, something Lauren thought she'd never find in a partner. Perhaps one of the best things about Justin is that he understands Lauren's need to abstain from alcohol, the importance sobriety plays in her present and future. Together they celebrate her milestones, goals and achievements. He respects her choices and freely allows her to embrace all that life has to offer, even though much of it remains well outside of his own comfort zone. After years of watching my daughter attempt to save the wounded men of the world, I'm grateful she's finally found love with a decent, caring individual.

CHAPTER NINETEEN

After the Hate

LAUREN_____

The 2017 Unite the Right riot in Charlottesville, Virginia, changed my life.

The death of Heather Heyer, the thirty-two-year-old paralegal and anti-racism activist, shocked but did not surprise me. James Alex Fields Jr was sentenced to life in prison with no chance of parole, but I knew this would happen again. And again. The violence, the "all means necessary" that is part of white power culture means this type of thing isn't a one-off.

What really burned me was hearing them call Heather "a fat, childless slut," hateful words very similar to those that had been thrown at me. I knew I needed to start making amends for the damage I had caused, to find a cause where I could give back, create change and feel good about myself. I decided to contact Life After Hate, a non-profit organization that helps individuals disengage from extremist violence, including ISIS. Run by former extremists, most of them from the far right, its mission is to inspire, educate and reform those wishing to disconnect from extreme ideology and become peaceful members of society. I soon received an email from Brad Galloway, a researcher and interventionist for the Organization for the Prevention of Violence, who wanted to talk with me before accepting my offer of help.

I was certain I'd come across this guy during my time in the movement. I introduced myself, sharing a bit about my past, and sure enough, Brad told me he'd left a few years before me. We had a great chat and soon after he added me to Exit USA, a website that acts as a bridge between those looking to exit the movement and the formers who help them. I wrote a shortened version of my story, posting it on their website for everyone to read.

I received a lot of compliments on my piece and on my recovery, and was soon messaged by Angela King, one of the directors of Life After Hate. She was well-spoken and gentle, and if I hadn't heard of her beforehand, I would never have guessed she'd once been a skinhead and enforcer. We compared our lives and I was struck by the similarities. Since we were both women who'd been involved in hatred, it made sense we'd have a lot in common. Angela added me to the larger Life After Hate network where I got to know many others on the same road as me. It was refreshing to be part of such a group, to meet new people and belong to such a great network after years of trying so hard to fit in. With them, I didn't need to change—they liked me as I was.

Within a month of becoming part of the group, Brad asked me to take part in several academic interviews to help researchers come up with methods to dissuade young people from joining the movement. It was nice to have different ways of getting my message out, new and interesting forums where I could help people, the total opposite of how I'd behaved while in white power. I'd found my passion: helping others re-create their lives without the movement.

My first interview took place during lunch at a local Boston Pizza restaurant. I was a bit hesitant because I didn't know the man and had never done an interview before, but once I was reassured my personal information would be withheld, I felt ready to begin. He started by saying, "I'm mainly interested in what drove you into hatred in the first place."

"My attraction to the movement," I told him, "wasn't so much about the ideology, but rather it was a cause I could attach my anger to."

My second interview was conducted over the phone (again, my name and personal information were kept confidential) as the researcher wasn't local. He seemed intrigued by everything I said, asking just the right questions to keep me talking for four hours. "Hey," he began when I brought up my binge-drinking, "can you tell me more about that?"

"I did it for the same reasons I got into the movement. I didn't like myself and I wanted to escape. I just got into the drinking first."

"How would you describe your identity at age sixteen?"

"I was a nobody," I replied.

"If there is one pivotal moment regarding your leaving the movement," he asked, "what was it?"

"Once, when I was up on stage at a concert, I couldn't seem to get the lyrics to the song out of my mouth. I knew them but I just couldn't say them."

I think he was especially pleased that I was able to explain everything that had been going on in my head back then.

Not long after, I received an email from another Life After Hate member, asking if I'd participate in a project with Dr. Barbara Perry, Director of the Centre on Hate, Bias and Extremism. When we connected, Barbara explained that she was writing an academic textbook. Along with several other participants, I was asked to write my story in my own words. Some of her questions included, How did you get into the movement? When did you start questioning yourself? And how did you get out? I started working on it immediately, planning to write one paragraph a day. Instead, I quickly realized how addictive writing can be, finishing my chapter within two weeks.

Barbara then asked me to attend an informal meeting with the other participants, so I took the day off work and drove to downtown Toronto. I wondered if I would meet any of my old friends down here. Who else might have exited the movement? In the meeting room sat two other former far-right extremists, some ex-street kids and former gang members—all of them from very different walks of life, but all coming from the same place as me. Most had been recruited as teens, aged fourteen to eighteen, and their time in each particular group varied from two years to ten plus. Many spoke of feeling alone, of searching for a sense of belonging, of wanting protection. I realized that when people talk about needing protection, deep down what they're actually in need of is protection from themselves. I never liked the person I was before the movement and that didn't change once inside it. Nothing was solved by excluding myself from society, keeping separate from people who didn't look like me. If anything, I wrote off many who could have helped me or been my friends. No two stories are the same, but there are always similarities.

In November 2018, Brad invited me to a conference in Edmonton called Partnering in Practice. By then, I felt I was finally ready for my first big public-speaking engagement but the six hours of travel —three on the plane, several more in security and endless lounges— without a cigarette nearly did me in. When I landed in Edmonton, my mom's friend and her husband picked me up and took me to dinner. She was the one who'd encouraged me to contact my mother all those years ago and clearly remembered the troubled kid I'd been. "We're so happy you're doing this," was the first thing they said as we sat down together. "We're really proud of you."

Conference participants were lodged in a boutique hotel in downtown Edmonton. I felt I was getting the royal treatment when I saw the room and huge king-size bed I had all to myself. I knew a few of the other participants: Brad, from Life After Hate, Amar, a researcher who'd interviewed me, and Ryan, the researcher whom I'd spoken with over the phone. Once I was settled, we met in the lobby and went for a late dinner. I was tired and not really hungry but there was no way I wanted to miss out on this new social atmosphere.

I was up at five the next morning to make sure I looked presentable, glad I'd brought something other than my usual T-shirts and skateboard shoes. I dressed carefully, styled my hair and sent a picture to my mom and Justin, who wished me luck. Then I hopped on the subway and headed for the University of Alberta.

It was only upon arriving that I realized how big the event was. Multiple presentations were running at the same time in two large conference halls, both packed with people from all over the world. I was nervous listening to the others who presented so many great points of view, hoping all the while I'd sound as polished as they did. I was scheduled to speak at the day's end so, during breaks, I spent most of my time running through my speech. When I finally stood in front of the audience at four o'clock, I was surprised to realize I hadn't needed the rehearsals. I looked out at the audience, noticing how each person was on the edge of their seat as I recounted my past. Some had tears in their eyes, others looked as though their jaws had dropped to the floor. I'd never understood the impact of a real-life story until that moment. And I never thought, in a million years, that I'd be sharing mine in front of hundreds of strangers. When I finished, most of the audience—about two hundred people—came forward to introduce themselves. I shook hands and accepted congratulations. Wow, I thought. I guess I did a good job.

A representative from Moonshot CVE, an organization working to halt online recruitment, introduced himself and told me they were working on a project called Canada ReDirect, a voluntary anti-radicalization program, initially aimed at individuals in danger of being recruited by terrorist organizations or criminal gangs, that has since evolved to help new Canadians and socially awkward youth. "It's an initiative that will redirect people searching for hateful online content to something more positive," he explained.

When he asked if I'd help, I agreed. Their preventative actions might not have saved me when I was first getting into the movement, but I might have benefited from a nudge in those moments when the little voice in my head had argued, "This isn't right." It's been a healthy journey for me because I've had to pore over all the negative shit I'd used to radicalize myself, scouring the old journals I'd kept while in the shelters—which I've since burned—and various emails to find the cracks where something, anything, could have helped prevent my entry into white power. Before those exercises, I'd never realized how often I'd done what every racist does: made exceptions. If I were out of sync with the subculture somehow, I would decide, I'm going to do this anyway. I just won't tell any of my friends.

In the past three years, along with counselling former white power members, I've assisted college students and researchers with their studies on hate. I've been interviewed for the *Washington Post*, *Toronto Sun* and *Toronto Star* newspapers and filmed for a CBC television segment. I hope by putting my story out there, people will start to understand hate—how people get drawn into it, how it recruits its victims, how it affects not only the person involved but their families and friends, and how it is possible to leave and start again.

In February 2021, I left my job in construction and became a full-time Outreach Specialist with ExitUSA.

JEANETTE

Charlottesville gave me a new perspective on white supremacy. I finally encouraged Lauren to open up about her experiences and former beliefs, and when she started talking, I started listening. Really listening, as I should have years ago. I hadn't realized how long it would take for her to leave it all behind, how much effort she'd need to put into changing her mindset before she could live her new life.

Our dialogue began with two books. I'd just finished reading *Small Great Things* by Jodi Picoult, a novel about a white supremacist, when Lauren asked for *Autobiography of a Recovering Skinhead—The Frank Meeink Story* for Christmas. I read it after she did and was amazed at how many of Frankie's experiences closely mirrored Lauren's. My voice was laced with astonishment as I asked, "Frankie talks about a lady named Angela King. That's not the same Angela you work with in Life After Hate, is it?"

Lauren laughed when she saw my face. "Yeah, that's Angela. She's cool."

"But she was an enforcer for the movement."

"Yeah, she was. Back then," Lauren admitted. "If you heard Angela was coming to see you, you knew you were in shit. But she's changed. Now she helps people."

"And Brad? This guy you've been talking to on the phone? Was he one of them too?"

"Yup," Lauren laughed. "He was in the movement too."

The more I read and questioned, the more I began to see these people—and my own daughter—as incredibly brave men and women who'd fallen on life's slippery path but were now assisting others to get their lives back on track.

During those turbulent times when racism was front and centre in her life, the best I could hope for was Lauren's survival. To hear her speak, to watch her slideshows, to see how far she's come and what she's doing with that knowledge is more than I could have ever asked for. I'm proud of the young woman she's become, thrilled that she uses her past experiences to further our understanding of extremism and vastly relieved she's been given this second chance.

CHAPTER TWENTY

In Retrospect

LAUREN

Back in high school, one of my teachers assigned us an essay in response to the gun control debate. I wrote that banning guns was only a Band-Aid solution, that the issues prompting their use needed to be addressed. "Guns are intended to have the trigger pulled," I wrote. "However, we aren't addressing where the illegal weapons come from or the core beliefs that lead someone to violence."

The teacher looked at my first sentence and, as the class listened in, said, "What? Lauren, really?" His voice and manner were both totally condescending, reminiscent of Poppa's treatment of me.

I tried to back up my viewpoint as best I could but his only response was, "You need to check your facts more thoroughly."

It would have helped if he had engaged with me and tried to understand my opinion, rather than blithely dismissing it based on the first sentence. The whole episode left me believing I wasn't being listened to; that, because my opinion differed from his, I was somehow wrong.

In retrospect, this pattern of being "talked to" as opposed to "talked with" did little to help me through school and life. It certainly didn't teach me to think critically. In fact, all it did was reaffirm my core belief that my opinion wasn't valued, that I wasn't important enough to be listened to, that I couldn't make my own decisions.

As I help formers deal with their choice to leave hate, I keep those early lessons in mind. When I first disengaged, I would have been grateful to have had another former to talk to. Now that I have the opportunity to assist others, I first try to get to know them as individuals—I'll ask how their week is going, what's new in their lives, and let them do most of the talking while I listen and try to understand what's driven them to this belief in the first place, so that I can help them look at others the same way. Listening, having an open dialogue, asking questions that challenge their mindset and core beliefs have, I believe, worked far better than arguing or shoving my opinions down their throats. I don't debate and I don't judge.

What I've found is that people need someone who'll make an effort to understand them, to see them as they really are, to show them the way out of hate. They don't need to feel more ostracized than they already do. I remember how difficult it was to leave my old life behind. I know there's no such thing as an overnight solution, that the process of disengagement is full of roadblocks. My own included not being sure of my identity, not wanting to be alone, being left without a set of beliefs and most of all, questioning my right to a future with someone. Who would want to date someone who'd been into extremism? I've learned so much, all of it the hard way, and feel it's vitally important to pass along my knowledge to others who are ready to leave hate behind.

Sitting at the other end of the table, I can say that it feels good to help someone transition out of hate, to make their path a little easier. I feel satisfaction when I see them make improvements to their own lives, so I'm prepared to do this for as long as it's needed, which I imagine will be for many years to come. Being involved in Life After Hate makes me feel I've contributed more to countering hatred than I ever contributed to the white power movement. Sharing my story is the most important thing I can do.

I've done a lot of soul-searching and what I've discovered is this: I was engaged in anger, in senseless fighting, hate and heavy drinking because I didn't want to face my own problems. Clearly, my own perceived inadequacies as a child had led to shame, which I tried to hide by acting out. The more I needed to hide, the more I acted out.

I dealt with verbal abuse and shaming by my grandfather and lost my father/best friend at the age of sixteen. I've forgiven Poppa, not because he deserved it but because I don't want to hold onto the negative energy anymore. I know my dad didn't want to go; if he'd had the choice, he would have stayed with us forever. He'll always be my dad.

I had opinions and principles I couldn't express. It was through white power that I felt able to show where I stood in the world, rightly or wrongly. I couldn't see the behaviours I disliked in other people in myself. I'd advocated for girls in the movement, thinking they'd be just like me, and I'd loved the praise and affirmation when the guys said, "There should be more girls like you." But when their misogyny was directed at me, their words no longer sounded like praise. Instead I began to see that no woman in her right mind would want the life I led. Between losing Tim and Jan, the false narratives of the subculture and the hypocrisy of being a female submerged in hate, I felt I had no choice but to leave white power behind. I finally made the decision to create a better life, to be genuine, to have real friends and healthy relationships.

Once upon a time, I shut myself off from those who could've helped me and instead responded to everything negative. There are times when I miss the danger and thrills of being in a gang but I've found healthier alternatives—bungee jumping, skydiving—anything that promises thrills and allows me to take pictures to share with my family (who think I'm nuts). All of these experiences leave me with good memories, unlike the many regrets I still hold from the past.

JEANETTE

In Brene Brown's TED Talks "The Power of Vulnerability" and "Listening to Shame," the renowned researcher says we have to be vulnerable in order to make human connections. Shame, she says, is the fear of disconnection, of not being good enough. It thrives in an environment of silence and judgment. To protect ourselves from shame, we numb our vulnerability, suppressing both good and bad emotions.

Lauren learned to numb her vulnerability early. From a young age she seemed unable to show empathy, her behaviour always defensive, always about her. We loved her as much as any parent can love their child, but we unwittingly reinforced her lack of self-esteem with both silence and judgment. The elder of two, we told her to "set a good example," "be a good girl" and "not talk back to your elders" even as she struggled to feel positive about herself. Paul thought he was showing her the depth of his love by helping her with her schoolwork, but Lauren thought she wasn't measuring up. My father's words and actions, his bigoted views and narcissistic personality made it clear that she had let him down. And while I'd long vowed never to be the parent he was, in some ways I was worse—I didn't stand up to his bullying and, by extension, became complicit. At school, peer pressure, teachers who singled out the quiet kids and school bullies all became relevant at the same time her emerging sexuality was creating its own confusion. And then her father died. I see now how the early roots of shame festered in Lauren—the sense that she wasn't good enough, pretty enough, smart enough, thin enough.

I wish I'd seen the similarities between the movement and my own family during that time. Outwardly both wished to be perceived as unified, but anyone who dared be different was thrown to the wolves. Both were characterized by infighting and jockeying for position. I'd been tossed away, as had my husband and kids, by my father because my older brother and his wife wanted attention for themselves. Lauren had been supplanted by another girl, lost her boyfriend, been de-patched and thrown out of her apartment by similar jealousies, all within the space of a few days. Yet both of us, equally strong-willed and determined, kept at it, trying over and over to fit in. If I'd had earlier insight, would it have changed things? Probably not, but who knows?

As loving parents, we did our best to protect Lauren from the evils waiting to prey on innocent little girls. In hindsight, I realize that we did a huge disservice to both Lauren and her brother by sheltering them. We neglected to give them the necessary skills to survive in today's world.

I asked Lauren recently if taking the internet away would have prevented her from becoming involved in the movement. "It would have reinforced my theories of mind control and the ideology of mind-crimes, where one is not allowed to think a certain way," she replied. "If you'd kept me off white power sites or away from the group, I'd have gone further underground."

"The way I see it," she continued with a shrug, "keeping troubled people from accessing information just pushes them into terror cells. That's how you get that one-in-a-hundred person who carries out mass shootings or killings."

It didn't help that I fell victim to the parenting stigma that prevents us from talking about the bad things our kids do for fear of being shamed or embarrassed, even though that's when we need support the most. Years after Lauren's self-harming, I confessed my humiliation and horror to a friend and one of my sisters-in-law, who then told me of similar experiences with their daughters. Think of the comfort and support we could have offered one another at the time.

The damage was done long before Donny came on the scene. When Lauren taught the daycare kids to swear, she had already shut down. Drinking to excess, self-harming—if she hadn't been involved in extremism, she would have found some other outlet for her pain, one equally as self-destructive. NSBM, metal music and the white power movement gave Lauren the freedom to express her anger, bitterness and discomfort, something that we had denied her.

Somewhat like childbirth, the years Lauren was involved with extremism are a blur of pain that seems increasingly remote. I truly believe we were lucky. While nightmarish at the time, her choices seem marginal now in comparison to the fates that often befall other lost youth. I think of her crews as people looking for acceptance, friendship and that sense of community we all want, not as hardened criminals, violent skinheads or neo-Nazis looking to annihilate another race. While they may have preached those ideals, few, I believe, actually practised them.

The strength of Lauren's will, so often the source of conflict, along with her intelligence and decency, helped her survive and eventually become the person she was always meant to be: confident, loving, funny. Part of our family but also part of a growing group of people dedicated to helping others escape from extremism.

I've never forgotten the advice I received when Lauren first left— keep the door open. Those words gave me hope when I thought I'd lost my daughter, strength when I wanted to crumble, responsibility when I wanted nothing more than to write Lauren off as a lost cause. They made me question my values, my role as a parent and my love, but more importantly, they begged me to ask myself, How could I ignore my own child, disown her as my father had me, just because she'd done something I hadn't agreed with?

I've learned to love my children unconditionally rather than imposing my values, my rules, my judgment upon them. I'm imperfect, I've made mistakes—why should I expect my kids to be any different? Sure, they do and say things that piss me off sometimes but at the end of the day, I still love them. All I can do now is hope the boundaries and tools I've given them will allow them both to fly solo.

Epilogue

LAUREN

Once I'd made up my mind to leave the movement, I was troubled by my remaining tattoos. Whenever I saw them, I was reminded of all of my past mistakes, ashamed of what I'd inked on my body. Eventually, I had two of them covered with more positive images that reflected who I'd become and who I wanted to be. The Celtic cross on my right arm was covered with an hourglass, vines and roses signifying how time heals. I covered my Odin's Rune with a candy skull and oak leaves, signifying my friends Tim and Jan.

In August 2019, my last hate tattoo, RAHOWA (Racial Holy War), perched on my upper back between my shoulder blades, was covered with a floral cathedral window design. My tattoo artist had drawn the design in an inverted V shape with the larger portion covering the old tattoo and the first hour of my session involved placement of the new artwork. I'd invited Justin, along with the CBC producer who'd filmed me in May and her cameraman, to watch and film as I bid farewell to my old life and the final reminder of hate I'd held onto for so many years. It was a relief to see that toxic ink gradually disappear. Now, at last, I'm free of that chapter of my life and everything that went along with it.

Acknowledgments

We've had the support of many wonderful people, through good times and bad. "Thank you" doesn't convey how immensely grateful we are for their love and assistance, but perhaps seeing their names in print will do the trick.

JEANETTE'S LIST

My wonderful mom—my support, my loving buddy throughout the whole darned thing. I miss you so much, every day.

My amazing son—I'm blessed to have you in my life.

Lisa—a lifetime of friendship and that one, tiny little email. Thank you for all of it.

Aisha—our first draft editor who, thankfully, "thinks too much." You are a blessing.

Regina's father—those magic words of hope: "Keep the door open." I will always be grateful.

Donna "Teach" Morrissey—wonderful mentor and dear friend.

The incomparable Ink Sistas and fabulous writers of the WCDR.

Our beta readers, Sherri, Channon, Joan, Lisa, Steve—you are stellar!

The amazing crew at Life After Hate. I'm honoured to know all of you and to be part of your wonderful organization.

Our photographers at One Tree Studio: you guys are the best!

A huge thank you to Lynn and Kilmeny from Tidewater Press, for your passion and insight, for taking a chance on our controversial tale and these two unproven writers.

My dearest Paul—wonderful father and husband. Guiding us, loving us from afar.

Lauren—I'm so grateful to have you back in my life. So proud to be your mom.

And to all who've picked up this book and followed our trek—may you never have to walk in our shoes.

LAUREN'S LIST

In loving memory of Jan Korinth (March 17, 2012)—the guy I shared my doubts with about the movement but more importantly the reason I'm walking free. It's rare to find a friend where you don't need to say anything to know what the other person is thinking and even more rare to find that friend in toxic circumstances. It's been years since you departed; however there hasn't been one milestone that I haven't wished I could share it with you, one moment of self-doubt where I haven't looked to you for encouragement or one funny moment where I know for a fact we wouldn't have died of laughter together. We may be lifetimes apart now, but I know we'll always walk side by side. Rest well, Jan, until we meet again.

In loving memory of Timothy Dean (January 1, 2010). I've tried and failed to find the words that seem like enough. The streets are never an easy thing to navigate or survive, however you made it one hundred times easier; you gave me the shirt off your back many times, both figuratively and literally. You had nothing to do with extremism but chose to see past my outer shell and bring out the person who was inside all along. I'll always remember your gentle nature and firm guiding hand, but more importantly the compassion you gave me when I least deserved it. There is no way I'll be able to pay you back for everything, but if I can pay forward even a small fraction of what you've given me then I will have done what I set out to do. Rest well, Tim, and thank you!

Organizations That Can Help

When our journey began, there were few online resources to help navigate the world of far-right extremism. Thankfully, information and support are available now for families dealing with a loved one's journey into and out of extremism. You don't have to go through this alone. The following organizations are currently studying, researching or assisting white power members in leaving the movement.

Life After Hate, *lifeafterhate.org*: Founded in 2011, Life After Hate's message is simple: "Life After Hate is dedicated to inspiring individuals to a place of compassion and forgiveness, for themselves and for all people." Formers themselves, their goal is to interrupt violence committed in the name of ideological or religious beliefs through education, intervention, research and outreach. They currently help people exiting hate groups and support those who've already left, in both the United States and Canada.

Exit USA, *lifeafterhate.org/exitusa*: Part of Life After Hate's outreach program, Exit USA was born in 2014 and is available to people around the world. Its mission statement reads, "No judgment. Just help. If you're ready to leave hate and violence behind, we're here to support you. At Exit USA we are dedicated to helping individuals leave the white power movement and start building a more fulfilling and positive life, just like we did."

We Counter Hate, *wecounterhate.com*: Under the Life After Hate umbrella, the #wecounterhate initiative on Twitter was launched to curb the spread of hate speech on the social media platform. The two-year campaign drastically reduced or deleted the number of tweets recognized as "hate." Many of those user accounts have been suspended.

The Canadian Anti-Hate Network, *www.antihate.ca*: An independent, non-profit organization made up of leading researchers and experts, their web page reads: "The Canadian Anti-Hate Network monitors and counters hate groups. Our work is already having an impact. We've exposed and shut down prominent alt-right neo-Nazi propagandists." They offer education and information on hate groups to the public, media, researchers, courts, law enforcement and community groups.

Anti-Defamation League, *www.adl.org*: Founded in 1913 by lawyer Sigmund Livingston, their mission statement reads: "To stop the defamation of the Jewish people and secure justice and fair treatment to all." This site gives useful education and resource information for the US, although there doesn't seem to be a Canadian version.

Anti-Racist Canada (ARC), *anti-racistcanada.blogspot.com*: An online blog tracking hate groups, whose mission statement reads: "A group of diverse but like-minded individuals, the members of ARC have come together in their common desire to fight hatred, bigotry, intolerance and violence because of the harm these antisocial behaviours cause to our society. In that effort, we will not use or sanction the use of illegal actions (such as violence or intimidation) in pursuit of our desired aims and if we learn of anyone who does use these unethical methods, we will report those individuals to the authorities. Instead, we will use the guarantees found in the Canadian Charter of Rights and Freedoms that ensure freedom of legal speech and expression." Useful for education and research, with a link to *antihate.ca*.

Against Violent Extremism Network, *againstviolentextremism.org*: One of Life After Hate's programs, along with Formers Anonymous and Strong Cities network, it is "a unique and powerful global force in the ongoing struggle to tackle violent extremism. Former violent extremists and survivors are empowered to work together to push back extremist narratives and prevent the recruitment of 'at-risk' youth."

Organization for the Prevention of Violence, *preventviolence. ca*: Based in Edmonton, Alberta, it is "a community and expert-led non-government organization. We are engaged in research and prevention-based activities that aim to mitigate hate-motivated violence. In pursuit of this goal, we work closely with communities, human service providers, and all levels of government."

Moonshot CVE, *moonshotcve.com*: Dedicated to working to disrupt and ultimately end violent extremism, the organization connects vulnerable individuals with counsellors. Canada ReDirect is a program developed through Moonshot CVE, aimed at redirecting people away from white power sites.

Centre on Hate, Bias and Extremism, *https://socialscienceandhumanities.ontariotechu.ca/centre-on-hate-bias-and-extremism/index.php*: The Centre on Hate, Bias and Extremism at Ontario Tech University in Oshawa, Ontario, "will be a magnet for high-quality academics who will contribute to the intellectual climate, locally and internationally. It will send a powerful message about our values while enabling the university to build its research capacity, share new knowledge and become the go-to source for policy developers seeking data, guidance and advice."